Dear Stephen -
We Shared Smiles
We wiped the tears
and through the years
our friendship has grown
along with us
you are truly a wonderful part of my life

Thank you for your friendship!
Have a Safe and fun trip!

RUMI: THE ART OF LOVING

Love
Niloofar

Jalâluddin Rumi

RUMI

THE ART OF LOVING

Edited and Translated by

Rasoul Shams

RUMI PUBLICATIONS
an imprint of
RUMI POETRY CLUB
2012

Rumi: The Art of Loving
Jalâluddin Rumi
Edited and Translated by Rasoul Shams

ISBN-13: 978-0-9850568-0-3
ISBN-10: 0985056800

Library of Congress Control Number: 2012901039

First Published in 2012
RUMI PUBLICATIONS
Rumi Poetry Club
P.O. Box 526239
Salt Lake City, UT 84152-6239
Email: info@rumipoetryclub.com
Website: www.rumipoetryclub.com

Cover painting and design by Setsuko Yoshida
www.setsukopaintings.com

Printed in the United States of America

The heart is a candle longing to be lit
and illuminate.
Torn from the beloved,
the tormented heart desires to be united.
Not knowing what longing and burning is,
you miss this:
Love cannot be learned or taught;
love comes as grace.

Rumi

CONTENTS

Part III. Compassion & Wisdom in Action
12+1 Stories from Rumi's Life

PREFACE

Rumi is one of the most widely-read poets today, and there are many anthologies of his poetry on the market. It is therefore appropriate to say a few words about the salient features of this new Rumi book.

This book is divided into three parts. Part I, "Understanding Rumi," presents two essays; the first on Rumi's life ("A Messenger from the Sun") and the second on Rumi's thought ("The Path of Love in the Ocean of Life"), which together provide a context through which to better appreciate his poetry. Such understanding of Rumi's cultural roots and poetic vision is important for both his translators and his readers. If Rumi's poetry is uprooted from its soil and atmosphere, it will wither away because of our mis-interpretations. For this reason, I have also included a glossary of terms and symbols in Rumi's poetry at the end of this book.

Part II, "The Rubaiyat of Rumi," contains 144+1 quatrains from Rumi. They are arranged into 12 topical chapters (each containing 12 quatrains): On the Pain and Joy of Longing; The Search; Who Am I?; The Beloved's Face; Die to Yourself; The Art of Living; Night Secrets; Water of Life; Fire of Love; Unity and Union; Peaceful Mind; and Rumi on His Life, Poetry and Death. In categorizing Rumi's quatrains into these twelve chapters, I had in mind the symbolism of twelve months in a calendar year. I have chosen from Rumi's quatrains, rather than from his long poems, to provide a small collection of poems in which each poem like a candle flame warms and illuminates our hearts whenever we happen to read it.

Part III, "Compassion and Wisdom in Action," recounts twelve stories from Rumi's life. Wisdom stories are found in all cultures and spiritual traditions, and are a remarkable feature of Sufi literature as well. The stories in Part III shed light on Rumi as a master poet who journeyed the path of love in the garden of his own heart as he also presents this spiritual journey with such elegance and ecstasy in his poetry.

This anthology is not a second-hand rendition or inspired version of Rumi's poems. It is an original translation from Persian, the language in which Rumi spoke and wrote. In this way, I hope, readers get glimpses of

Rumi's poetry as he intended. I have used free-verse in plain English to render a faithful and yet a clear translation. How far this effort is valid and useful, the reader is the best judge of it.

In selecting the poems for this volume, I have used authentic sources and printed editions of Rumi's works to ensure that they are indeed Rumi's poems, not the quatrains added later by scribes to the Rumi manuscripts. The Persian sources and references for all the poems translated in this volume have also been cited.

Over the years, I have noticed that many of Rumi's fans and readers in English also want to read and hear the Persian sound and cadence of his poems as they were originally rhymed and musical. For this purpose, I have added the Persian text (in English script) of each quatrain under its translation.

In researching, writing, and translating this book, I have tried to take a scholarly approach to ensure its accuracy and documentation. Nevertheless, this book is not a technical treatise; it is primarily a Rumi anthology for the general public. The information and poems contained in this volume are meant for people who want to read inspirational words of love and wisdom from the pen of a master poet and sage but applicable for their own life journey.

And finally, a personal note: I was first exposed to Rumi's poetry in my Persian classes as a young boy growing up in Iran, historically called Persia. Even after I left Iran more than three decades ago, the poetry books of Rumi and several other Persian poets have been my spiritual companions, and I have enjoyed reading and reflecting on them. In recent years, I have watched with delight the growing popularity of Rumi – thanks to the free-verse translations of his poems widely available now (although with varying degrees of quality and accuracy). As many scholars have opined, Rumi's poetry is a vast, deep ocean; we therefore need more translators to bring out the gems hidden in his poems. The writing and translation of this Rumi anthology was made gradually over a period of five years; it is a labor of love and an outcome of my poetry meditation. I hope you will enjoy reading and be inspired by this small but timeless garland from Rumi.

Thank you for your fellowship!

Rasoul Shams
September 30, 2011 (Rumi's birthday)

Part I

UNDERSTADING RUMI

"We cannot exhaust man's being in knowledge of him."

Karl Jaspers in *Way to Wisdom* (1954)

"The most beautiful experience we can have is the mysterious. It is the fundamental emotion which stands at the cradle of true art and true science."

Albert Einstein in *Ideas and Opinions* (1954)

I have reached a meadow
wherein love grows.
Whatever dirt is brought here
becomes all clean and pure.

Rumi

Divân-e Shams
Ode #583: 6174

A MESSENGER FROM THE SUN

A Sketch of Rumi's Life

Since I am a devotee of the Sun
I speak of sunshine only.
I am not of the dark night, nor a night-worshiper
I shall not interpret your dreams.
I am a messenger from the Sun
I am His interpreter only.
And this is how I do it:
Secretly, I ask the Sun
Then I answer your questions.[1]

Rumi

There is a famous story from Rumi's life: When he was a small boy, he chanced to meet the renowned Persian poet Attâr who told the boy's father: "Not far in the future, this boy will kindle the souls of lovers all over the world." In his life time, Rumi was a well-known and respected Islamic teacher, Persian poet and Sufi master. He lived most of his life in Anatolia or the Eastern Roman (Byzantine) kingdom, called *Rum* in Persian; hence the name *Rumi*. After his death, Rumi's poetry and reputation spread through a vast part of the Orient where, for centuries, he has been known as Mowlânâ or Mawlânâ (Mevlânâ in Turkish), meaning "Our Master." Interestingly, this general title for an eminent sage, scholar or poet has become an honorific pseudonym for Rumi. If the story of Rumi's meeting with Attâr is true, one wonders what Attâr saw in the young Rumi's personality to make such a remarkable prediction. Are great artists born, as we have often heard? If so, why did it take over thirty five years for Rumi to start composing his fiery poems? Here I do not want to speculate on the general issue of genius. What I hope to provide in this chapter is some key information about Rumi's life so that readers better appreciate his poetry. In writing this chapter, I have consulted both historical sources and modern studies on this subject.[2]

From Balkh to Konya

Rumi's given name was Jalâluddin Mohammad and he was the youngest child of his family. Historical sources place his birth on September 30, 1207 in the city of Balkh (in present-day Afghanistan) which was then a political, economic and cultural center in the eastern part of the Persian kingdom. Through centuries, Balkh was a hub for various spiritual traditions including the Zoroastrian, Buddhist, and Islamic faiths. Rumi's father, Bahâ Valad, was a Muslim preacher and mystic, and indeed his first teacher. We are fortunate to have Bahâ Valad's book of discourses (*Ma'âref-e Bahâ Valad*) [3] which had an enormous impact on Rumi's thinking.

When Rumi was a young boy, his family decided to leave Balkh and emigrate westward. Two reasons have been given for this emigration. First, Bahâ Valad in his speeches often criticized philosophers because they based their understanding of truth merely on logical, verbal arguments, and ignored spiritual practice and the realm of the heart. Such criticisms surely hurt the feelings of the powerful philosophers, such as Fakhruddin Râzi (1149-1209), who were friends with Sultan Mohammad Khârazm-Shah, the ruler of the Persian kingdom in Balkh. The king himself, who sometimes attended Bahâ Valad's sermons, apparently did not like the growing group gathering around a pious, mystic preacher who kept distance from the court. Loyalists to the king and the philosophers' camp may thus have intimidated Bahâ Valad in Balkh. The second reason for Bahâ Valad's departure from Balkh was that as a widely-traveled preacher who met people from various walks of life, he became alarmed by the rise of Genghis Khan as an ambitious, powerful leader and his imminent threat to the unpopular Khârazm-Shah.

In about 1219, Rumi's family left Balkh. About three hundred people were in Bahâ Valad's caravan. They travelled along the historical Silk Road and stopped at the city of Nishâbur in northeast Iran where the poet Attâr lived. This was the occasion when Attâr supposedly met Bahâ Valad's family and was so impressed by Jalâluddin that he presented the young boy with a copy of *Asrâr Nâmeh* ("The Book of Secrets") – a book Attâr had composed during his own youth. Although the story of this meeting is not recorded in Rumi's earliest biographies and appears in later literature[4], we know for certain that Rumi was an avid reader of Persian poetry. He was especially fond of Sanâ'ii, who died in 1131, and Attâr, who was killed in 1221 when the

Mongol army massacred the people of Nishâbur. Indeed, Rumi viewed his work as a continuation of these poets' legacy.

Bahâ Valad and his family were in Baghdad in 1221 when the Mongols sacked Balkh and Nishâbur, and massacred their inhabitants. After making a pilgrimage to Mecca, Bahâ Valad and his companions moved to Anatolia (Asia Minor). In the thirteenth century, Anatolia was ruled by the Seljuq Dynasty who had conquered the Byzantine kingdom two centuries earlier. The Seljuqs were of Turkish origin, but over time had blended with the Persians, converted to Islam, and whose courts were supporters of Persian poets and Sufi masters. In the town of Lâranda (today's Karaman in southwest Turkey), Rumi's mother, Mo'mene Khâtun, died; her tomb still exists there. In 1224, the eighteen-year-old Rumi married a hometown girl – Gowhar Khâtun – whose family had accompanied Bahâ Valad's westward sojourn. The couple soon had two sons: Alâ'eddin (born in 1225 and died in 1262, long before Rumi), and Sultân Valad (born in 1226 and the one who became Rumi's successor).

In 1228, Bahâ Valad and his family settled in the nearby city of Konya at the request of the Seljuq king Sultan Alâ'eddin Kaygobâd. Konya, once an ancient Greek city called Iconium, was then the Seljuq capital where people of various religions, languages, and ethnicities lived in peace. A religious school was built in Konya for Bahâ Valad where he held his classes and sermons.

In 1231, Bahâ Valad died at the age of 80. Rumi took over his father's position as the head of the family and the school, but he still needed to complete his education. A year later, Burhânuddin Termezi, who was a disciple of Bahâ Valad and who had tutored the young Rumi back in Balkh, came to Konya and undertook a systematic training of Rumi in various fields of learning as well as the Sufi spiritual path. In 1233, Rumi was sent to Aleppo and Damascus (both cities now in Syria) to study Islamic disciplines with eminent teachers of the day. Seven years later, Rumi returned to Konya. A scholar *par excellence*, Rumi became a popular preacher and teacher in Konya with hundreds of students and followers. His wife Gowhar Khâtun died, probably in 1240. A year later, his teacher Burhânuddin, who lived in the nearby town of Kayseri, passed away; his tomb is still a historical monument there. Rumi inherited his library.

Shortly thereafter, Rumi married Kera Khâtun, a widow from Konya who had a son (and possibly a daughter named Kimya) from her previous marriage. This second marriage brought two more children to Rumi's family: A son named Mozaffar-eddin Amir Âlem, who died in 1277; and a daughter named Malakeh Khâtun, who died in 1306. Rumi's descendants from the line of Sultân Valad still live in Turkey and are called Chelebis. (Chelebi is a Turkish title meaning "an honorable person").

A Poet is Born

November 29, 1244 was a second birthday for Rumi. On that day, he met Shams Tabrizi in one of Konya's bazaars. Shams, literally meaning "Sun," was a wandering dervish born in Tabriz, a city in northwest Iran. He had led a long life of traveling and studying with Sufis. When they met in Konya, Shams was possibly about 60 and Rumi was 37.

In their very first meeting, Rumi and Shams were impressed by each other's spiritual insight. Subsequent conversations and retreats with Shams (a Sufi tradition called *Soh'bat* or "conversation") drastically changed Rumi's lifestyle and perspective. He was transformed from a scholar to a mystic, from a preacher to a poet. Of course, Rumi himself was ripe for this spiritual transformation; he had been prepared by his father Bahâ Valad, by his teacher Burhânuddin, and by the Persian mystic poets he had read so voraciously. After meeting Shams, Rumi became detached from books, reduced his teaching schedule, and instead, spent most of his time on prayer, meditation, poetry, *samâ* (listening to music) and "whirling dance." This was later developed by his son Sultân Valad as a practice of the Whirling Dervishes.

The nature of the relationship between Rumi and Shams has puzzled Rumi readers for centuries. Had Rumi and Shams not met, we probably would not have had Rumi's poetry; nor would we ever have known of Shams. Shams acted as a catalyst; he removed the cap rock from the volcano of Rumi's heart and hence the fiery poems of love and ecstasy poured from Rumi's tongue and pen. Shams was an enigmatic figure. His extant discourses (*Maġâlât-e Shams-e Tabrizi*)[5], probably written down by Sultân Valad, portray Shams as a widely-traveled man with deep knowledge of the Sufi tradition. However, Rumi's disciples resented Shams, partly because they felt that he had kidnapped their teacher from them and partly because of Shams' blunt character. In March 1246, Shams left Konya for Damascus in protest of the disciples' mistreatment of him; Rumi dispatched his younger son to bring him back. In April 1247, Shams returned to Konya, but after a while the same problems surfaced. In January 1248, Shams disappeared for good. Nobody knows what happened to him or where he went. Some scholars believe that Shams was killed by Rumi's angry disciples and that even Rumi's elder son Alâ'eddin was involved in this matter. Other scholars, however, doubt this story as well as the authenticity of the tomb in Konya presently attributed to Shams. In any case, Shams' disappearance devastated Rumi. He went to Damascus twice to look for Shams, but finally concluded that Shams was within him. In the years to come, Rumi found two other soul brothers for "conversation" (*soh'bat*): Salâhuddin Zarkub, a goldsmith and a former disciple of Burhânuddin Termezi, who died in 1258; and Husâmuddin Chelebi, a young disciple of Rumi from Konya's chivalry class, who died in 1284.

Rumi's Legacy

Rumi's works, all in Persian, are divided into prose and poetry. His prose works include (1) *Fihi Mâ Fihi*[6] ("In It What Is In It") and (2) *Majâles Sab'a*[7] ("Seven Sermons"), both of which are Rumi's discourses and public lectures scribed by Sultân Valad; and (3) *Maktubât*[8] ("Letters"), a collection of 144 letters Rumi wrote to his friends, family members, disciples or government officials in Anatolia.

Rumi's poems (98 percent in Persian and about two percent in Arabic) are collected in two books, and the English anthologies of Rumi's poetry available on the market today are selections from the following two works:
(1) *Divân-e Shams*[9] ("The Poetry Book of Shams"), also called *Divân-e Kabir* ("The Great Book of Poetry") or *Kulliyât-e Shams* ("Collected Works Dedicated to Shams"), contains over 3200 lyric odes (*ghazal*) and over 1800 quatrains (*rubâi'yât*). This book is full of ecstatic love poems. Persian poets who compose *ghazal* usually end their poems with a pen name (in the last line of the poem). In the *Divân-e Shams*, Rumi sometimes uses the pen-name of *Khamush* ("Silent") but in many others he cites the name of Shams.
(2) *Masnavi-ye Maa'navi*[10] ("Rhyming Couplets on Spirituality") is a six-volume book of didactic poetry (teaching stories) which Rumi recited to Husâmuddin Chelebi during the last decade of his life.

Rumi died on December 17, 1273 at age 67. Aflâki reports that people from diverse religions and ethnicities – Muslims, Christians, Jews, Persians, Turks, Arabs and Greek, the rich and the poor, the elite and the illiterate, women and men – all came to his funeral and mourned the loss of their beloved poet and spiritual teacher. Buried in Konya, Rumi's tomb (now called Mevlana Museum, but traditionally known as the "Green Dome," or "Yâshil Turbe" in Turkish, "Gobbat ul-Khadhra" in Arabic, and "Gonbad-e Sabz" in Persian) has been a shrine for centuries. It is visited by thousands of curious travelers, poetry lovers, and Sufi pilgrims each year. Every December 17 in Konya is celebrated as *Shab-e Arus* or *Shab-e Urs* ("wedding night," symbolizing reunion with the Divine) in the spirit of Rumi's will that those who come to his tomb should not cry and grieve, but rejoice with prayer, poetry, music, dance, and contemplation.

Rumi was not a poet by profession. He earned his living from public-funded teaching and religious services. Yet, he is one of the most prolific Persian poets of all time. Over a period of three decades, he composed about 70,000 lines of rhymed poetry, in highly musical rhythms and with rich images.

Rumi was born on Sunday and died at sunset on Sunday. Interestingly, the eight hundredth anniversary of his birth in 2007, which was celebrated worldwide, also fell on Sunday. Rumi's closest spiritual friend was named Shams ("Sun") and the words "Sun" (*shams, khorshid*) and sunshine (*aftâb*) have a remarkable presence in Rumi's poetry. This symbolism of the Sun is elegantly consistent with the place of Rumi among us. For seven centuries, his poetry and vision has shined like the bright, warm Sun upon the minds and hearts of those who have read him. Master Rumi is an enlightening poet for all generations.

Rumi Comes to America

Rumi has come into the Western consciousness and culture through several ways: Accounts of travels to Konya; scholarly works on Persian literature or Sufism; Sufi spirituality of the so-called Whirling Dervishes; and translation of his poetry. John Porter Brown, a native of Ohio who served as U.S. diplomat in Constantinople (Istanbul) and knew Arabic, Persian and Turkish, published in 1868 a fascinating and informative book *The Dervishes or Oriental Spiritualism*. He died in Istanbul in 1872 and was the first Orientalist in the United States Foreign Service. English travel writer and folklorist Lucy Mary Jane Garnett (1849-1934) also popularized the lore of the Whirling Dervishes in her 1912 book *Mysticism and Magic in Turkey: An Account of the Religious Doctrines, Monastic Organization, and Ecstatic Powers of the Dervish Orders*.

English translations of Rumi's poetry were first made by several British scholars in the late nineteenth and early twentieth centuries: Sir James Redhouse (1811-1892), Edward Henry Whinfield (1836-1922), Edward Granville Browne (1862-1926), Reynold Alleyne Nicholson (1868-1945), and Arthur John Arberry (1905-1969). Their scholarly translations still constitute the foundation of Rumi's poetry in English.

Nicholson, in particular, devoted his life to the study and translation of Rumi's poetry and vision, and remains to this day one of a handful of authorities on Rumi. Nicholson was Browne's student and successor at Cambridge University. His first book *Selected Poems from the Divân-e Shams-e Tabrizi* was published in 1898. In the introduction to this book, Nicholson introduced Rumi as "the greatest mystical poet of any age" and remarked:

> In sublimity of thought and grandeur of expression he challenges the greatest masters of song; time after time he strikes a lofty note without effort; the clearness of his vision gives a wonderful exaltation to his verse, which beats against the sky; his odes throb with passion and rapture-enkindling power; his diction is choice and unartificial.

Nicholson single-handedly accomplished the heroic task of not only producing a scholarly edition of the *Mathnawi of Jalaluddin Rumi* from various Persian manuscripts, but also translating the entire book into English and writing detailed commentaries to it. The result was an 8-volume work published from 1925-1940. At the end of his translation, Nicholson had this to say:

> Familiarity does not always breed disillusion. To-day the words I applied to the author of the *Mathnawi* thirty-five years ago, 'the greatest mystical poet of any age,' seem to me no more than just. Where else shall we find such a panorama of universal existence unrolling itself through Time into Eternity? And, apart from the supreme mystical quality of the poem, what a wealth of satire, humour and pathos! (Volume VI, p. ix).

Arberry was Nicholson's student and successor at Cambridge. In the introduction he prepared for Nicholson's posthumous book, *Rumi, Poet and Mystic* (1950), Arberry wrote:

> In Rumi the Persian mystical genius found its supreme expression. Viewing the vast landscape of Sufi poetry, we see him standing out as a sublime mountain peak ... To the West, now slowly realizing the magnitude of his genius, ... he is fully able to prove a source of inspiration and delight not surpassed by any other poet in the world's literature.

The current fascination with Rumi is partly due to free-verse translations of his poetry which make Rumi accessible to the general public. A pioneer in this field is Coleman Barks. Born in 1937 in Tennessee, Barks studied at the University of North Carolina and the University of California in Berkeley. He taught English poetry and creative writing at the University of Georgia for three decades. Barks' attention was drawn to Rumi by his poet friend Robert Bly who, during a poetry meeting in 1976, gave him a copy of Arberry's book and said, "These poems need to be released from their cages." Barks does not know Persian; he uses literal translations made by Nicholson, Arberry or by his American-Iranian friend John Moyne and then does "second translations" or renditions of Rumi's poems in the free-verse style of poets like Walt Whitman, Gary Snyder, and Mary Oliver. In this way, he has presented a flavor and fragrance of Rumi in the dozens of anthologies and audio-records he has produced over the past three decades. His book, *The Essential Rumi*, has been a best-selling poetry book in North America since it was first published in 1995. Apart from Barks, several other scholars, poets, translators, and Sufi authors have popularized Rumi's poetry in North America and Europe since the 1980s.

Rumi is popular today also because of his remarkable personality: He integrated in his person the learning of a scholar, the insight of a sage, the compassion of a saint, and the art and imagination of a poet. Rumi's vision quenches our thirst for meaning, joy, love, peace; his poetry offers spiritual solutions to the many grave problems of our life and society. And Rumi appeals because, as he believed, each one of us carries a memory, no matter how faint, of our divine home, and each one of us hears, no matter how infrequently, the song of the celestial bird inhabiting the garden of our heart.

The poet digs a creek
to send water to the following centuries.
Although each age has its own voices,
the words of the by-gone poets are helpful as well.[11]

Rumi

Bibliographical Notes

Rumi's poems cited in this chapter are my translations from the following Persian sources:

Divân:
Kulliyât-e Shams-e Tabrizi: Divân-e Kabir, by Mowlânâ Jalâluddin Mohammad Balkhi Rumi, edited by Badi al-Zamân Foruzânfar (10 volumes, 1957-1967, Tehran University Press; reprinted by Amir Kabir Press, Tehran, 1976).
Masnavi:
Masnavi-ye Maa'navi, by Mowlânâ Jalâluddin Mohammad Balkhi Rumi, edited by Reynold Nicholson (8 volumes, 1925-1940, London); Persian text printed in one volume by Amir Kabir Press, Tehran, 1971.

1. *Divân, ghazal* #1621: 6966-67
2. Shamsuddin Ahmad Aflâki (who died in 1365) in the *Manâĝeb al-Ârefin* ("The Virtuous Acts of the Mystics") compiled the life stories of Rumi as well as those of Rumi's father (Bahâ'uddin Valad), his teacher (Burhânuddin Termezi), his spiritual friends (Shams Tabrizi, Salâhuddin Zarkub and Husâmuddin Chelebi), his son (Sultân Valad), and his grandson (Ulu Amir Âref). Aflâki had access to Rumi's books as well as to his family members and friends. Unfortunately, in several cases, Aflâki gives contradicting versions and dates for important events, making it difficult to know which narrative is true. This book, critically edited by

Tahsin Yazichi, was published in two volumes in Ankara (2nd edition, 1976 & 1980; reprinted in Tehran, 1983). Aside from this important source, I have also used the Iranian scholar Badi al-Zamân Foruzânfar's *Resâleh dar Ahvâl va Zendegâni-ye Mowlânâ Jalâluddin Mohammad* ("Treatise on the Life of Master Jalâluddin Mohammad," in Persian; Tehran, 1954, 2nd edition), Annemarie Schimmel's *The Triumphal Sun: A Study of the Works of Jalaluddin Rumi* (London, 1978; State University of New York Press 1993, 2nd edition), and Franklin D. Lewis' *Rumi, Past and Present, East and West* (Oxford, 2000).

3. Bahâ'uddin Valad, *Ma'âref* ("The Teachings"), edited by Badi al-Zamân Foruzânfar, 2 volumes (Tehran, 1954 & 1959; reprinted, 1973). A very partial translation is by Coleman Barks and John Moyne, *The Drowned Book: Ecstatic and Earthy Reflections of Bahauddin, the Father of Rumi* (San Francisco, 2004).

4. This story is mentioned in the *Tazkerat ul-Shu'arâ* ("Biographies of the Poets") by Dowlatshâh Samarġandi who lived in the fifteenth century (some two hundred years after Rumi); it is not found in the earlier biographies of Rumi. Dowlatshâh Samarġandi, *Tazkerat ul-Shu'arâ*, edited by Mohammad Abbâsi (Tehran, 1958); in Persian, no English translation is available.

5. Shamsuddin Mohammad Tabrizi, *Maġâlât-e Shams-e Tabrizi* ("The Discourses of Shams Tabrizi"), edited by Mohammad Ali Movvahed, 2 volumes (Tehran, 1990). An English translation from the Persian (with the contents re-arranged biographically) is by William Chittick, *Me and Rumi: The Autobiography of Shams-i Tabrizi* (Louisville, KY, 2004). Another complete translation (from the Turkish translation) is by Refik Algan and Camille Adams Helminski, *Rumi's Sun: The Teachings of Shams of Tabriz* (Louisville, KY, 2008).

6. Mowlânâ Jalâluddin Mohammad Balkhi Rumi, *Fihi Mâ Fihi* ("In It What Is In It"), edited by Badi al-Zamân Foruzânfar (Tehran University Press, 1951; reprinted by Amir Kabir, Tehran, 1969). Two English translations are available: *Discourses of Rumi* by A. J. Arberry (London, 1961); *Signs of the Unseen: The Discourses of Jalaluddin Rumi* by W. M. Thackston (Boston, 1999).

7. Mowlânâ Jalâluddin Mohammad Balkhi Rumi, *Majâles Sab'a* ("Seven Sermons"), edited by Ahmad Ramzi, Valad Chelebi, and Feridun Nâfezbek (Istanbul: 1937); edited by Towfiġ H. Sob'hâni (Tehran, 1996). In Persian; no English translation is available.

8. Mowlânâ Jalâluddin Mohammad Balkhi Rumi, *Maktubât* ("Letters"), edited by Ahmad Ramzi and Feridun Nâfezbek (Istanbul, 1937); edited by Towfiġ H. Sob'hani (Tehran, 2001). In Persian; no English translation is available.

9. Mowlânâ Jalâluddin Mohammad Balkhi Rumi, *Kulliyât-e Shams-e Tabrizi*: *Divân-e Kabir*, edited by Badi al-Zamân Foruzânfar, 10 volumes (Tehran University Press, 1957-1967; reprinted by Amir Kabir Press, Tehran, 1976). Partial translations of the *Divân-e Shams* include Reynold Nicholson's *Selected Poems from the Diwân Shams Tabrizi* (Cambridge University Press, 1898; Bethesda, MD, 2001 reprint), and A. J. Arberry, *Mystical Poems of Rumi* (University of Chicago Press, 2008 reprint). Rumi's lyric odes (*ghazals*) have been translated into English by Nevit O. Ergin from the Turkish translation (by Abdulbaki Gölpinârli, 1957-58) and published in 22 volumes (various publishers, 1995-2003). Rumi's quatrains (*rubâiyât*) have been translated by Ibrahim Gamard and Rawan Farhadi, *The Quatrains of Rumi* (San Rafael, CA, 2008).

10. Mowlânâ Jalâluddin Mohammad Balkhi Rumi, *Masnavi-ye Maa'navi* ("Rhyming Couplets on Spirituality"), or *Mathnawi of Jalaluddin Rumi*, edited, translated and commentaries by Reynold Nicholson, 8 volumes (London, 1925-1940); the Persian text was published in a single volume by Amir Kabir Press (Tehran, 1971). Partial translations include: *Teachings of Rumi: Masnavi*, by E.H. Whinfield (London, 1889; reprinted 1979); *Tales from the Masnavi* and *More Tales from the Masnavi* by A. J. Arberry (London, 1961 and 1963).

11. *Masnavi*, III: 2537-38

THE PATH OF LOVE IN THE OCEAN OF LIFE

The Poet's Voice & Vision

Go and wash off all hatred from your chest,
seven times with water, like one washes dishes.
Then you can become our companion,
drinking from the wine of love.[1]

Rumi

Rumi was a poet in love with All, the Universe, the Source, the Mystery, Beauty, Life, and Art. His mind and language were finely tuned to his heart – a spiritual realm brimming with joy, compassion, longing, grief, ecstasy, peace, insight, meaning, and mystery. To his avid readers, Rumi appears to be a contemplative poet who trusts existence, treasures life, and offers a positive view of the human's place in the world. For all these reasons, people from various cultures, languages, and centuries can relate to Rumi's voice because he is so vast and inclusive like an ocean, and so simple and essential like water. Moreover, the joyous, compassionate and peaceful vision embedded in his poetry makes it a much needed message for our divided, violent, and stressful world.

Rumi's poems are filled with expressions of love, beloved, friend, kindness, tenderness, beauty, joy, grief, separation, longing, heart, wine, drunkenness, selflessness, God, truth, union, and unity. But, we have to understand these terms in the context of his poetry. Love is a key to comprehending Rumi's mind because it is a common thread that runs through all of his poems, directly or by implication. The intensity of the language and the elegant, ecstatic imagery that Rumi employs to express the path of love is rarely seen in other poets. It is thus important to have a right view of what Rumi means by love. Sometimes we use the word love for a strong feeling of liking someone or something. However, this desire may as well be centered on our ego or based on a give-and-take business relationship in which the calculating head, not the illuminated heart, is involved. Such love can also easily turn into frustration and hatred, because both those emotions are two sides of the same coin – selfishness and greed. Love, in Rumi's vision, *is* when the ego or carnal self (*nafs*) is *naught*; and such love is realized when the heart is open and the mind is awakened to the reality of life beyond the fictional ego.

Rumi often confesses that love cannot be defined in clear-cut words or analyzed by the rigid logic of the head:

Whatever I say to describe and explain love,
when I come face to face with love, I am embarrassed by my statement.
Although verbal explanation clarifies the matter,
love not verbalized is even clearer.[2]

To understand love, one must experience it:

Someone asked: What is love?
I said: Don't ask about its meaning.
You will see when you become "we."[3]

Poetry, at best, can speak of love in metaphors:

Love is to fly heavenward.
Love is to rend a hundred veils with every breath.
Love is to see beyond what the eye sees.
Love is to run joyfully in the alleys of the heart.[4]

The poet immersed in the light and warmth of love sees its signs and effects everywhere:

O God, this love
        how hidden it is
        how visible it is.
It is like the moon; it is like wine.
O God, this love has decorated
        our life and the universe.[5]

Rumi, following a Sufi teaching, views love (*eshg*) on two levels: (1) The real source of love or True Love (*eshg-e hagigi*) which is of God, Truth, Ground of Being, Creator or by whatever name we want to use; (2) Love derived from the Source, or Derivative Love (*eshg-e mojâzi*) which is the reflection of the Divine or True Love in all beings.

In the realm of the Unseen,
there is sandal wood burning.
This love is the smoke of that incense.[6]

In Rumi's view, "Love is God." This is the same as the saying "God is Love." If A is equal to B, then B is also equal to A. Logically and mathematically these two statements are the same, but for practical and psychological reasons, Rumi does not start from abstract theology; instead, he starts from love – a quality intimate and common to all humans. Rumi thus approaches the Divine, the Sacred and the Mystery through love. His is the path of love (*tarigat-e eshg*). In one of his poems, Rumi says that "*the path of the Derivative Love leads to True Love,*" and that "*the culmination of human love is with Rahmân (the mercy and bliss of God).*"[7] That is why Rumi does not draw a rigid boundary between the Divine love and human love toward fellow humans or other creatures; because love, in its true sense, is a reflection of the Divine love in our hearts.

This realization of love is achieved through two processes: (1) "Transcending" the small, suffering self (ego) and being free from its endless dreams and its dualistic thinking – us versus the rest, this versus that; (2) "seeing" the beauty, grace, glory, and oneness of God in the entire creation including human life. Sufis call the first process *fanâ* ("die to yourself," or "die before your die") akin to the Buddhist notion of nirvana. The second stage is called *baqâ*, "eternal life" in the presence of the Beloved, the Ground of Being. Rumi uses the symbolism of wine and drunkenness to describe the ecstasy of melting into the love, beauty, mystery, and presence of God; one who drinks from this spiritual wine transcends the ego and identifies one's own being as one with All. Out of this union, a vast and deep sense of love emerges in the poet's heart.

Love for Rumi was a heart-felt reality and an outcome of his deep meditation on the nature of life and existence. Such a view of love is shared by the mystics and spiritual poets of various cultures, religions, and languages. They see love, like the force of gravity, embedded in the very matrix of the cosmos and life. Rumi says:

If the Sky were not in love,
*   its chest would not be pure and shining.*
If the Sun were not in love,
*   its face would not be beautiful and bright.*
If the Earth and mountains were not in love,
*   no plant could sprout out from their heart.*
If the Sea were not aware of love,
*   it would have remained motionless somewhere.*[8]

Love is what moves life; love is what holds the universe together. That is why the mystic poet sees God (the alpha, the omega, the source, and the sustainer of existence) in the light of love which is everywhere and eternal. God is the master lover; (S)He is also the beloved. Therefore, Rumi's notion of universal love is not something abstract, aloof, and impractical, but alive, rich, and relevant to our daily life. It was indeed the source of Rumi's own poetry. Through love the perishable particle partakes in the eternal; through love we join the dance of the cosmos and sing the song of God. The Iranian scholar Ali Dashti once remarked: "When I am engaged in the reading of the *Divân-e Shams*, I feel like orbiting around a distant star – a world far nobler, more inclusive, and more expansive than the atmosphere of this earthly world. In that world, stars are like living beings talking to you. One gets closer to an eternal and all-inclusive spirit pulsating in the infinite space." [9]

Love is alchemy; it has a transforming power over whatever it touches. Love does not solve our problems the way our ego desires; the problems are simply dissolved in the alchemy of love:

Through love bitter things become sweet.
Through love bits of copper turn into gold.
Through love dregs taste like pure wine.
Through love pains are healed. [10]

While the calculating head may come to a dead end, the heart always finds a way out of darkness to light:

Reason says:
> *These six directions are the limits.*
> *There is no way out!*
Love says:
> *Oh yes, there is a way.*
> *I have traveled it many times.*
Reason sees a market and begins to trade.
Love sees wonderful bazaars beyond this market. [11]

Love gives us a creative, joyous life beyond our small, illusionary self. In the following poem, Rumi speaks of his own experience:

I was dead: I became alive.
I was sobbing: I became laughter.
The glory of love came upon me,
and I became the everlasting glory. [12]

Of course, the path of love is not smooth, straight and without hardship:

In love, there is union and separation
This path has its ups and downs.[13]

The path of love is narrow; it is paved with the blood of devotion and the sweat of hardwork because reining in one's ego is the most difficult affair in life. However, the path itself leads the wayfarer. Rumi says that as you are an active seeker, the beloved is also looking for you:

There is no lover seeking union
without the beloved searching for him, too.
A thirsty person cries for fresh water;
while water is crying: "Who wants to drink me?"[14]

Rumi extends the scope and function of love from a personal level to international and interfaith relations. Love is the essence and object of every true religion; that is why:

The religion of love is separate from all forms of religions.
Lovers are of one nation and one religion: God.[15]

If Rumi's vision is valid, one may rightly ask, how come all this hatred, violence, and sufferings in the world and in the history of humankind? The answer, according to all sages, is simply this: Ignorance and greed. Rumi illustrates this point in a simple parable in the *Masnavi*.

> Four men traveling together were given one *dirham* (a silver coin) to buy whatever they desired on their journey. These men spoke different tongues; when the time came to spend the coin:
> The Persian said, "I want *Anghur*."
> The Arab said, "I want *Enab*."
> The Turk said, "I want *Uzum*."
> And the Greek said, "I want *Estafil*."
> The men began to quarrel, each pushing his desired case until a wise man, who knew all their languages, told them that those four words meant the same thing: Grape.[16]

This parable characterizes the nature of a vast majority of human conflicts, whether among individuals or among religions and nations. Every group places itself at the center of the world and is firmly attached to its own wishes and icons with little understanding of other peoples, and without a sense of compassion or a spirit of cooperation.

Every human wants to eat from the "the grape" of life – to live a happy and fulfilled life. As long as our wants are the real needs and we put our intelligence and compassion to work, God's world has sufficient "coins" to provide for our life. A Persian proverb says: "Two worldly kings cannot be contained in one country, but ten dervishes can sleep on a single carpet." When we go into the inner meanings of phenomena and understand the transient and interconnected nature of life, our attention will not be limited to our endless selfish desires and our effort will not be directed toward unnecessary hostility and violence over symbols, appearances, and names. Rumi says, *"Conflicts among people come from their attachment to names. When they go into meanings, peace prevails."*[17]

True peace is a consequence of inner development, heart-felt understanding, and compassion. But can this mystic love be translated into social action and everyday life? Erich Fromm ended his book *The Art of Loving* exploring this question. He expressed faith in "the possibility of love as a social not only exceptional-individual phenomenon" because love "is the ultimate and real need in every human being." Some may argue that aggression, violence and hatred are powerful forces in humans as well. There is no doubt about this; history provides ample evidence. But mystics and sages suggest that human nature is fundamentally goodness and love, and that hatred and violence are afflictions. Children normally have good, caring hearts, and as they grow up and see sufferings in their society and lives, they dream of what should be done and what they can do to make the world a better place for all. When Jesus Christ said that "until you become like little children, you will not enter the kingdom of heaven" (Matthew, 18:3), he was referring to this pure, angelic nature of humans. Society is a collection of individuals and their relationships; therefore, the way we behave and act determines the state and fate of our society. If, as mystics and spiritual masters say, love is the fundamental truth of existence, then it is possible that through the inner journeys of individuals and their collective effort and sharing, our society is built on the basis of understanding, compassion, joy, and creativity because all these qualities at their best stem from love. Therefore, Fromm's idealism, as he concluded *The Art of Loving*, is rooted in "the insight into the very nature of man." Interestingly, Fromm also refers to Rumi as "a man of profound insight into the nature of man," who "discussed the nature of the instincts, the power of reason over the instincts, the nature of the self, of consciousness, the unconscious and cosmic consciousness."[18]

I am that Moon that shines in a placeless universe.
Do not seek me outside;
I abide within your very soul and life.
Everyone calls you towards himself;
I invite you to yourself.
A poem is like the boat; its meaning like the sea:
Come onboard at once!
Let me sail this boat![19]

Rumi

Bibliographical Notes

Rumi's poems cited in this chapter are my translations from the following Persian sources:

Divân:
Kulliyât-e Shams-e Tabrizi: Divân-e Kabir, by Mowlânâ Jalâluddin Mohammad Balkhi Rumi, edited by Badi al-Zamân Foruzânfar (10 volumes, 1957-1967, Tehran University Press; reprinted by Amir Kabir Press, Tehran, 1976).

Masnavi:
Masnavi-ye Maa'navi, by Mowlânâ Jalâluddin Mohammad Balkhi Rumi, edited by Reynold Nicholson (8 volumes, 1925-1940, London); Persian text reprinted in one volume by Amir Kabir Press, Tehran, 1971.

1. *Divân, ghazal* #2131: 22549
2. *Masnvai,* I: 112-13
3. *Divân, ghazal* #2733: 29050-51
4. *Divân, ghazal* # 1919: 20201-02 & -05
5. *Divân, ghazal* # 95: 1059-60
6. *Divân, ghazal* #2949:31322
7. *Divân, ghazal* #27: 336 & 338
8. *Divân, ghazal* #2674: 28369-28372
9. Ali Dashti, *Seyri dar Divân-e Shams* (Jâvidân Press, Tehran, 1958) p. 20. [In Persian]
10. *Masnavi,* II: 1529-31
11. *Divân, ghazal* #132: 1521-22
12. *Divân, ghazal* #1393: 14742
13. *Divân, ghazal* #2442: 29156
14. *Masnavi,* III: 4393-97
15. *Masnavi,* II: 1770

16. This parable is in the *Masnavi*, II: 3681-90
17. *Masnavi*, II: 3680
18. Erich Fromm in the Introduction to Reza Ârâsteh's *Rumi, The Persian Poet: Rebirth in Creativity and Love* (1965).
19. *Divân, ghazal* #1518: 15976-77 & -85

Part II

THE RUBAIYAT (QUATRAINS) OF RUMI

144 +1 Poems on the Art of Loving

"Man – of all ages and cultures – is confronted with the question of how to overcome separateness, how to achieve union, how to transcend one's own individual life."

Erich Fromm in *The Art of Loving* (1956)

"[Rumi] calls us, as he called his friends for seven centuries, to participate in the dance that moves through the universe, to circle around the Sun of Love."

Annemarie Schimmel in
I Am Wind, You Are Fire (1992)

If you have no beloved,
why do you not seek one?
If you have found your beloved,
why do you not rejoice?

Rumi

Divân-e Shams
Ode #3061: 32589

ABOUT THIS TRANSLATION

Rumi's language was Persian. To better appreciate his poetry, it may be useful to have some knowledge about his language. Today, Persian is the official language in Iran (where locally it is called Farsi), in Afghanistan (Dari), and in Tajikistan (Tajiki). This is a population totaling about 110 million. Persian is also spoken in parts of Uzbekistan, Pakistan, Bahrain, Kuwait, and Iraq, and by several millions of Iranian and Afghani expats living in Western countries. In former times, Persian was more widely spoken in Central Asia, Caucasus, Middle East, and the Indian Subcontinent. In Rumi's time, during the Seljuq Dynasty, Persian was the court language in Konya, and it was spoken along with Turkish, Greek, and Arabic in Anatolia.

Persian belongs to the Indo-European family of languages, and shares common roots with Sanskrit, Greek and some European languages. Therefore, it should not be surprising to come across some Persian words having striking similarity with their English equivalents; for example *to* (thou), *tâ* (to), *dou* (two), *ast* or *hast* (is), *hastam* (am), *mâdar* (mother), *pedar* (father), *dokhtar* (daughter), *barâdar* (brother), *setâré* (star), *sepahr* (sphere), *tundar* (thunder), *bus* (kiss), *mush* (mouse), *gâw* (cow), *jangal* (jungle), *abruw* (eyebrow), *bad* (bad), *behtar* (better), *târik* (dark), *râst* (right), *na* (no), *nâm* (name), *now* (new), *dar* (door), and so on. After the invasion of the Persian Empire by the Muslim Arabs in the seventh century, and over the course of several centuries, a large number of Arabic words entered Persian and via that language, these words later entered Turkish and Hindustani vocabulary.

Poetry in Iran has a long history, going back to Zoroaster's songs (*gatha*), about three thousand years ago. What is today understood as Persian poetry includes a large corpus of verse produced by numerous poets over the past twelve centuries. Rumi is among the top five Persian poets of all time; the other four being Ferdowsi (920-1020), Omar Khayyam (1048-1131), Saadi (1209-1292), and Hâfez (1325-1389). In his genre of poetry, called *she'r-e erfâni* (spiritual or mystical poetry), Rumi followed in the footsteps of Sanâ'ii (1080?-1131) and Attâr (1130?/1145?-1220), and this poetic tradition was continued by Hâfez, Jâmi (1414-1492), and many other poets down to our time.

Classical Persian poetry comes in various forms. The *rubâ'ii* (plural: *rubâ'iyât*), an Arabic word meaning "quatrain," consists of four lines in which the first, second and fourth lines end with a given rhyme; the third line may or may not rhyme. Consider, for example, the following Persian quatrain from Rumi (poem #103 in this volume):

(1) eshǵ az azalast o tâ be abad khâhad bud
(2) juuyande-ye eshǵ bi-adad khâhad bud
(3) fardâ ke ǵiyâmat âshekârâ gardad
(4) ey har ki na âsheǵ ast radd khâhad bud

This poem consists of four lines or "hemistitchs" (*misra'* in Persian); two successive hemistitchs make up one "distitch" (*beyt*) or verse. "khâhad bud" (shall be) is the rhyme in lines 1, 2 and 4. The *rubâ'ii* in Persian is also sometimes called *tarâneh* (snatch) or *do-beyti* (double-verse).

A thirteenth-century manual on Persian poetry[1] states that one day the poet Rudaki (?859-940) was walking in the city of Ghazneh (in present-day Afghanistan) and saw several boys playing marbles with walnuts. One of the boys said, "*ghaltân ghaltân hami ravad tâ lab-e gu*" ("Rolling, rolling, it is going towards the pit"). Rudaki loved the poetic rhythm of this saying so much that he adopted it as a basis for the *rubâ'ii* poetry in Persian. Many scholars, however, believe that the *rubâ'ii* as a genre of folk poetry dates back to Pre-Islamic Persia.

Much like the Japanese *haiku*, the *ruba'ii* is a very short verse used to express strong emotions and brisk inspirations rather than a chain of thoughts and images. The best known work of Persian quatrains to the Western readers is, of course, *The Rubâ'iyât of Omar Khayyam*, which was translated into English verse by Edward FitzGerald (1809-1883). This book became highly popular and spread both Khayyam's and FitzGerald's fame on both sides of the Atlantic.

Rumi composed about 1800 quatrains which are included as the last part of his *Divân-e Shams* (or *Divân-e Kabir*). I have selected 144 of these quatrains for this volume and arranged them into 12 topical chapters, each containing 12 quatrains. The number 12 is obviously related to the symbolism of twelve months in the solar calendar as our planet circles the Sun.

I should also mention a few words about the sources of these quatrains. The *Divân-e Shams* was composed in a period when printing technology did not exist; books were then written by scribes on large sheets of paper. There are several manuscripts of the *Divân-e Shams* written by various scribes and calligraphers through the centuries. In due course, some scribes added a number of quatrains which are absent in the older manuscripts. For this reason, I have used authentic copies of the book to ensure that these poems are from Rumi.

Badi al-Zamân Foruzânfar (1900-1970), a renowned Rumi scholar from Iran, made a comparative study of several manuscripts of the *Divân-e Shams*, including the oldest manuscripts, and produced a scholarly edition with footnotes and indexes. This work was published in 10 volumes by Tehran University Press from 1957-67; it was also reprinted by Amir Kabir Press in Tehran in 1976. I have used this edition. To cross-check my selection of the quatrains, I then consulted a printed edition of the Konya manuscript, which is one of the oldest and most complete manuscripts of the *Divân-e Shams* written in 1367-68. This manuscript is kept at the Mevlana Museum in Konya, and it was recently printed, with scholarly footnotes and indexes by Towfiġ Sob'hâni, in two volumes in Tehran in 2007 on the occasion of the eight-hundredth anniversary of Rumi's birth.

I mention these bibliographic details here because most of the Rumi anthologies available on the market today have used a certain edition of the *Divân-e Shams* which is not authentic, especially with respect to its quatrains. This edition was published in one volume by Amir Kabir Press in Tehran in 1962 and has been reprinted numerous times. Many translators of Rumi have mistaken this book to be the one edited by Professor Foruzânfar because it contains an introductory chapter on Rumi's biography taken from one of Foruzânfar's books. However, that particular volume was not edited by Foruzânfar but was based on a nineteenth-century Indian print of the *Divân-e Shams* which obviously contains additional quatrains not found in Foruzânfar's edition or in the Konya manuscript. The arrangement and numbering of the quatrains in the Amir Kabir-Indian edition is also different from that of Foruzânfar's edition. The total number of the quatrains in the Amir Kabir-Indian edition is 1995, while in Foruzânfar's (University of Tehran's) edition there are 1983 and in the Konya manuscript there are 1863 quatrains. (Foruzânfar admitted that even his edition contained several non-Rumi quatrains, and he intended to write an essay about this issue. Unfortunately, his death in 1970 did not permit it.)

Translation is not an easy task, especially that of poetry which is a highly condensed and metaphorical form of writing. At one extreme, a word-by-word translation with scholarly explanations would make the poem too boring and dull to the general reader. At the other extreme, distortions, additions, omissions, and interpretations freely made by the translator will transform the original meaning and content of the poem. I have avoided both these extremes and have strived to present Rumi's poetry as he intended to the best of my knowledge. I have used free-verse contemporary English familiar to our generation. I feel that using plain English is also a sincere approach to Rumi's poetry because Rumi himself used commonly spoken and written Persian for his poetry.

Persian is a gender-neutral language. The word "uu" (pronounced as in *foo*t) means both "he" and "she." Even the word "God" has no gender association in Persian (unlike Arabic, English and many other languages in which "God" is masculine: He, His, and Him). Similarly, words like friend, beloved, etc. in Rumi's poetry have no gender associations. This makes it difficult to translate these words into English. I have used "he" or "she" depending on which one sounds more natural in that particular poem in English.

Since these poems are quatrains, I have used four lines for each poem to convey its original format as well. However, when a line became too long in English, I divided it into a main line followed by a sub-line.

Despite my best efforts, I do not claim these translations to be the best. Rumi's poetry is a deep and vast ocean. Each translator brings something of Rumi to the table, some translators more than the others. If this small Rumi anthology conveys a fair part of what Rumi composed, I shall consider the purpose of this publication fulfilled.

1. *Al-Mu'jam fi Ma'âyir Ash'âr al-Ajam* (in Persian), "A Book on the Scales of Persian Poetry," by Shams'uddin Muhammad ibn Ġays Râzi at about 1233 A.D. (edited by Muhammad Qazvini and Edward G. Browne, London, 1909).

TRANSLITERATIONS OF PERSIAN WORDS

Persian writing is at least 2500 years old, as evidenced from the stone inscriptions of the Iranian kings preserved in Persepolis, southwest Iran. Like the other historical languages, Persian has changed through time and has utilized several scripts. Initially, during the Achaemenid Dynasty (about 550-330 BC), Old Persian was written in the cuneiform script borrowed from Mesopotamia where writing itself was invented about five thousand years ago. In later times, the language adopted other scripts including Greek (after Alexander's invasion of Iran in 334 BC), Sogdian (during the Parthian Dynasty, 274 BC to 224 AD), and Pahlavi (Middle Persian script derived from the Aramaic script – the language Jesus Christ spoke) during the Sassanid Dynasty (224 to 651 AD). For the past twelve centuries, New Persian has been written in the Arabic script. A person unfamiliar with these languages and judging from the script alone may think that Persian and Arabic are the same languages. However, Persian has a different grammar, vocabulary, and history from that of Arabic. Arabic and Hebrew belong to the Semitic family of languages; Persian, as noted before, belongs to the Indo-European languages. The present Persian alphabet consists of 32 letters, 28 of which are common to Arabic, but four letters (*p*, *ch*, *zh*, *g*) are absent in Arabic. In turn, some Arabic letters are pronounced differently in Persian; for example *th* as in *think* is pronounced *s* in Persian (hence the Arabic word *Mathnavi* is pronounced *Masnavi* in Persian).

In this book, along with the English translations of Rumi's quatrains, I also present the Persian readings of the poems in English script. The following is a guide to transliterations of the Persian words used in this book.

PERSIAN VOWELS	ENGLISH SOUND	
â	art, father	
a	am, cat	
e	bed, pet	
i	inn, sin	
ii	bee, knee	long vowel i
o	go, no	
oo	goat, boat	long vowel o
u	push, book	
uu	boom, too	long vowel u

CONSONANTS	SOUND	
b	book, cab	
ch	cheese, catch	
d	door, dad	
f	fan, gift	
g	good, bag	
gh	Française	French "r"
ǵ	strong g	Absent in English[1]
h	holy, hat	
j	jar, gem	
k	keep, book	
kh	Bach	German ch
l	lady, tool	
m	man, name	
n	noon	
p	pet, tap	
r	room, free	
s	Sun, cycle	
sh	shape, dish	
t	tool, put	
v	very, vast	
y	you, buy	
z	zig-zag	
zh	vision	French j

Also note the following:

(1) ...-**e** (as in "Ketâb-**e** Rumi") means "of" ("Book of Rumi").

...-**ye** (as in "Siine-**ye** Rumi") means "of" ("Chest of Rumi").

-**e** comes after a consonant; -**ye** after a vowel.

(2) ... **o** ... which comes between two words is usually pronounced "**va**" in prose, but in poems it is pronounced "**o**" (as in "man o to"); it means "and" ("I and you").

(3) ...'... is a short pause on a given letter. Example: man'made

(4) When a consonant is repeated, it means that the letter should be pronounced strongly as if it were two letters. Two English examples are: o**ff** and bu**zz**.

1. The symbol **ǵ** (strong **g**) adopted in this book is the same as **q** that scholars use in their transliteration of the Arabic-Persian vocabulary. However, the common reader, unaware of this academic code among the scholars, pronounces **q** as **k**. In this way, *Quran* has become *Koran* in English while the actual pronunciation is *ǵur'an* (with a strong **ǵ**). I have avoided the use of this misleading **q**, and feel that **ǵ** better renders the original pronunciation of the letter.

(1)

ON THE PAIN AND JOY OF LONGING

1

I put my heart on this hazardous road
and unshackled it to follow you.
The wind brought me your scent.
In gratitude, I scattered my heart to the wind.

> *bar rah'gozar-e balâ, nehâdam del râ*
> *khâss az pe-ye to, pây goshâdam del râ*
> *az bâd marâ, buu-ye to âmad emruuz*
> *shokrâne-ye ân, be bâd dâdam del râ*

2

The night I see you in my dream, I know
when day comes, my heart will be restless.
Like the elephant who at night
          dreamed of his homeland India
and broke his chains in daylight.
          Who has the power to rein that elephant?

> *ân shab ke torâ be khâb biinam, peydâst*
> *chon ruuz shavad, cho ruuz del por ghoghâst*
> *ân piil ke duush khâb-e Henduustan diid*
> *az band bejast, tâğat-e ân piil kerâst?*

3

When I look at my beloved, she becomes shy.
If I don't see her, she tortures my heart.
Tonight, in the pond of her face
      the moon and stars are shining.
Without her water, I will be drained and turn into mud.

> *dar yâr nazar konam, khajel migardad*
> *var nangeramash, âfat-e del migardad*
> *dar âbe-e rokhash setâregân peydâ-and*
> *bi âb-e vey, âbam hame gel migardad*

4

When you come to my mind, my heart starts to pound
and tears of longing drip from my eyes.
Wherever I go and hear news from you,
my poor heart wants to fly out of my body toward you.

> *yâd-e to konam, delam tapiidan giirad*
> *khuunâbe ze diidegân chekiidan giirad*
> *har jâ khabar-e duust rasiidan giirad*
> *bichâre delam ze tan pariidan giirad*

5

My heart is in turmoil to the point of bubbling
      in order to reach your ecstasy.
It has lost its own consciousness
      to gain your consciousness.
The heart even wishes to drink poison
      if that is the only way to drink from your nectar.
It has molded into an earring
      in order to have access to your ear.

> *mijuushad del, tâ be juush-e to rasad*
> *bi'huush shodast, tâ be huush-e to rasad*
> *minuushad zah'r, tâ be nuush-e to rasad*
> *chon halġe shodast, tâ be guush-e to rasad*

6

If even a single particle of the heart is present in the chest,
life will be tormenting without you.
In the long chain of your beautiful hair,
   there are curls within knots.
A wise man caught in one of them becomes love-mad.
  If he doesn't, he isn't wise.

> *dar siine-ye har ke, zarre-ii del bâshad*
> *bi-esh'ĝ-e to, zedegiish mosh'kel bâshad*
> *bâ zolf-e cho zanjiir gereh' bar gereh ast*
> *divâne kasi bovad, ke âĝel bâshad*

7

I am madly in love with you.
  What good is advice and preaching?
I have drunk the killing water of love.
  What good is a little sugar?
They say, "Put chains on his feet."
The madness is in my heart.
  What use is the chain on my feet?

> *dar esh'ĝ-e to'am, nasiihat o pand che suud?*
> *zah'râb cheshide'am, marâ ĝand che suud?*
> *guuyand marâ ke: band bar pâsh nehid*
> *divâne del ast, pâm bar band che suud?*

8

With every moment of longing,
  the beloved tortures my sick heart.
Either she does not know how I feel,
  or her heart is made from stone.
I have written the story of my heart with tears of blood.
The beloved sees it, but doesn't read it.

> *har dam del-e khaste râ beranjânad, yâr*
> *yâ sang delast, yâ nemidânad yâr*
> *az diide be khun nabeshte-am, ĝesse-ye khiish*
> *mibiinad o hiich bar nemikhânad, yâr*

9

Curse me no more. I am already drunk from your curses,
drunk from your tasteful wine, fallen to the ground from so much joy.
Even if you give me bitter water, I will drink it like sugary juice.
So devoted, so devoted I am to you.

dosh'nâmam made, ke mast-e dosh'nâm-e to'am
mast-e sagat-e khosh-e khosh âshâm-e to'am
zah'râbe biyâr, ta benuusham cho shekar
man râm-e to'am, râm-e to'am, râm-e to'am

10

If you are a sea, I am your fish.
If you are a meadow, I am your deer.
I am a reed flute on your lips.
Blow into me. I love your breath.

gar daryâyii, man mâhi-ye daryâ-ye to'am
var sah'râyii, âhuu-ye sah'râ-ye to'am
dar man midam, bande-ye dam'hâ-ye to'am
sornâ-ye to'am, sornâ-ye to'am, sornâ-ye to'am

11

You're gone, and in my longing I shed tears of blood.
This ever-increasing grief of you makes me cry more.
No, I'm not saying it right! When you left, my eyes went after you.
Since my eyes have gone with you, how can I cry?

rafti vaz raftan-e to, man khuun migeryam
vaz ghosse-ye afzuun-e to, afzuun migeryam
nay, khod cho to rafti, pe-ye to diide beraft
chon diide beraft, baa'd az ân chun geryam?

12

Three things you've taken away from me, and so selectively:
>Patience from my heart,
>Color from my face,
>Sleep from my eyes.
So quick and sharp you are! Such hands as yours
cannot be conceived even in imagination.

>>*se chiiz az man be-borde-ii be-goziide*
>>*sabr az del o rang az rokh o khâb az diide*
>>*châbok dasti ke dast o bâzuut dorost*
>>*tasviir-e oǧuul, chon to nâzâyiide*

(2)

THE SEARCH

13

Within your living being, there is a spirit. Search for it!
In the mountain of your body, there is a jewel. Search for it!
O, wandering Sufi! If you are looking for it,
don't seek it outside; it is to be found within you.

> *dar jân-e to jâniist, bejuu ân jân râ*
> *dar kuuh-e to, dorriist, bejuu ân kân râ*
> *Sufi-ye ravande, gar to ân mi'juuyii*
> *biiruun to majuu, ze khod bejuu to ân râ*

14

The world in all its six directions is filled with God's light.
But people ask, "Where is *that* light?
A novice looked for it everywhere, left and right.
He was told: "This moment, look, without left or right."

> *goftand ke: shesh jahat hame nuur-e khodâst*
> *faryâd ze khalg khâst kân nuur kojâst?*
> *bigâne nazar kard be har suu, chap o râst*
> *goftand: dami nazar bekon, bi chap o râst*

15

O, clever mind, go away! This place is not for cleverness.
Even if you become thin as a hair, there is no room for you.
This is daylight; any lamp you light up
will be disgraced in the presence of sunshine.

> *ey aĝl boro, ke âgeli injâ niist*
> *gar muuy shavi, muuy-e to râ gonjâ niist*
> *ruuz âmad o ruuz har cherâghi ke forukht*
> *dar sho'le-ye âftâb joz rosvâ niist*

16

Daylight, come out! All particles in the world desire to dance.
Our souls too want to dance joyfully, footloose and with abandon.
And that great Dancer who has caused the heavens to whirl,
I will whisper to your ear where He shall dance.

> *ey ruuz, bar â, ke zarre-hâ raĝs konad*
> *jân'hâ ze khoshi, bi sar-o pâ raĝs konad*
> *ân kas ke azuu charkh o havâ raĝs konad*
> *dar guush-e to guuyam ke kojâ raĝs konad*

17

O those who are engaged in prayers in your own sanctuary,
the home is still far away; move on this very moment!
O those who are drowned in the affairs of the tavern,
a hundred caravans have passed by; you are still asleep.

> *ey ahl-e monâjât ke dar mehrâbiid*
> *manzel duur-ast, yek zamân beshetâbiid*
> *vey ahl-e kharâbat ke dar gharg-âbiid*
> *sad gâfele bogzasht o shomâ dar khâbiid*

18

O pious seekers who are wandering in the world:
Why are you perplexed by a mental idol?
What you are seeking the whole world for,
seek within yourself. You are already that.

ey ahl-e safâ ke dar jahân gardâniid
az bahr-e boti cherâ chonin heyrâniid?
uu râ ke shomâ dar-in jahân juuyâniid
dar khod cho be-juuyiid; shoma khod âniid

19

It is good that each day we halt in a new lodge
        and leave the old one behind,
like water flowing and free from stagnation.
Yesterday is gone; so is yesterday's tale.
Today, we have this new adventure.

har ruuz khosh-ast manzeli bespordan
chon âb-e ravân fâregh az afsordan
dey raft o hadis-e dey chon dey ham bogzasht
emruuz hadis-e tâze bâyad kardan

20

In the streets of your own mind, what are you seeking?
Why are you washing your eyes with tears of blood?
From head to toe, you are possessed by Truth.
Yet, you remain so ignorant of yourself: What else are you seeking?

dar ku-ye khyâl-e khod che mi'puuyii to?
vin diide be khuun-e del, che mi'shuuyii to?
az farg-e sarat tâ be gadam, hagg dârad
ey bi'khabar az khiish, che mi'juuyii to?

21

You search for one who can untie your knots.
      Yet, you die in that illusion.
You were born in the bosom of union.
      Yet, you die in separation.
You reside on a river bank.
      Yet, you sleep with thirst.
You sit on top of a treasure.
      Yet, you die a beggar.

ey dar talab-e gereh' goshâyii morde
az vasl bezâde, dar jodâyii morde
ey bar lab-e bahr, teshne dar khâb shode
vey bar sar-e ganj, az gedâyii morde

22

You have severed our relationship,
      but I do not despair.
You have chosen another lover,
      but I do not despair.
As long as I live, your grief will be my food.
There is much hope even in hopelessness;
      I do not even despair.

nomiid niyam, garche ze man bobridii
yâ bar sar-e man yâr-e degar bogzidii
tâ jân dâram, gham-e to khâham khordan
besiyâr omiid hast dar nomiidii

23

If your quest is the soul's home, you are that soul.
If your search is for a loaf of bread, you are that bread.
If you know this *secret*, you know *the* secret:
That you are seeking, you are that.

gar dar talab-e manzel-e jâni, jânii
gar dar talab-e loğ'me-ye nâni, nânii
in nokte-ye ramz agar bedâni, dânii:
har chiiz ke dar jostan-e âni, ânii

24

O my heart, what adventure are you seeking?
I am already with you if that is me you are seeking.
If you haven't seen the Beloved, who are you looking for?
If you have seen the Beloved, who else are you looking for?

ey del, che hadis o mâjerâ mi'juuyii?
man bâ to'am ey del, ar marâ mi'juuyii?
var zânk nadiide-ii, ke râ mi'juuyii?
var zânk bediide-ii, che râ mi'juuyii?

(3)

WHO AM I?

25

For some time, imitating others, I preferred myself above all.
Blind to my real self, I could hear my name only.
Trapped in my little self, I did not appreciate who I was or was not.
When I came out of myself, I saw my true being.

> *yekchand be taģlid goziidam khod râ*
> *nâ-diide hami nâm shaniidam khod râ*
> *dar khod budam, zân nasaziidam khod râ*
> *az khod cho beruun shodam, bediidam khod râ*

26

Sometimes I used to say: *I'm a king!*
And other times I would cry: *I'm a slave!*
That time has passed, and I no longer take this "I" for granted.
I have concluded: *"I" am not the conclusion.*

> *gah migoftam ke man amiir-am khod râ*
> *gah naa're zanân ke man asiiram khod râ*
> *ân raft, az in pas napaziiram khod râ*
> *begereftam in ke man nagiiram khod râ*

27

There is a path from your heart to mine.
My heart knows how to find it.
The heart is clear and fresh as water.
Pure water is a trusty mirror for the beauty of the moon.

> *ey jân, ze del-e to bar del-e man râh ast*
> *vaz jostan ân, dar del-e man âgâh ast*
> *ziirâ del-e man cho âb-e sâfi-ye khosh ast*
> *âb-e sâfi, âyiine-dâr-e mâh ast*

28

My dear soul, do you know who your Beloved is?
My lonely heart, are you aware of your dear Guest?
My lazy body, much as you seek a way out by every trick,
there is One who still drags you on the Way.
See who is the One seeking you?

> *ey jân, khabarat hast ke jânân-e to kiist?*
> *vey del, khabarat hast ke mehmân-e to kiist?*
> *ey tan ke be har hiile rahi mi'juuyii*
> *uu mi'keshadat, bebin ke juuyân-et to kiist?*

29

I am not concerned with to be or not to be.
I am detached from them both. Yet, *that* is not bravery.
The wonders in my heart don't drive me crazy.
This is bravery and the real madness!

> *bâ hasti o niisti-yam, bi'gânegist*
> *vaz har do boridanam, na mardânegist*
> *gar man ze ajâyebi ke dar del dâram*
> *divâne nemishavam, ze divânegist*

30

The One who sees both the outer and the inner
watches over the lovers in a hundred ways.
Look at your eye; see how the eye sees:
Who is the One who looks out from the inside?

> *ân chiiz ke bíiruun o daruun mi'negarad*
> *dar ahl'e jonuun, be sad fonuun mi'negarad*
> *dar díide negar, ke díide chuun minegarad*
> *vân kist ke az daruun beruun minegarad*

31

This human form that you see so well built
is an image fashioned in the Stable of Sorrows!
It sometimes looks like a demon, sometimes an angel,
        and sometimes a wild beast!
Who knows what a talisman this human bundle is?

> *in suurat-e âdami ke dar ham bastand*
> *naghshiist ke dar tavile-ye gham bastand*
> *gah' div-o gahi feresh'te vo gahi vah'shi*
> *in khod che telesmist ke bar ham bastand?*

32

The secrets of spiritual truth shall not be revealed by your questions,
nor by abandoning your position and possessions.
Devote your eye and heart to the blood-paved path of love.
Debating with your head will not lead you to illumination.

> *âsrâr-e haġiġat nashavad hall, be so'âl*
> *ney nüz be dar bâkhtan-e heshmat o mâl*
> *tâ díide vo del khuun nakoni panje sâl*
> *az ġal, kasi râ nabovad râh be hâl*

33

When your chest is washed clean from the ego,
you will see your true self and your first love.
You cannot see your own face without a mirror.
Look at the Beloved; He is your mirror.

chon pâk shod ze khodi-ye to, siine-ye to
khod-bin gardi, ze yâr-e diiriine-ye to
bi âyiine ruuye khüsh natvâni düd
dar yâr negar, ke uust âyiine-ye to

34

You have come from a heavenly home.
You have an idea of the pure world you belong to.
Alas! You only see your image in this clay form.
That is how you have forgotten your origin.

ey ânk-e to bar falak vatan dâshte-ii
khod râ ze jahân pâk pendâshte-ii
bar khâk, to naġsh-e khüsh benegâshte-ii
vân chiiz ke asl-e tost, bogzâshte-ii

35

Neither I am me, nor you are you, nor you are me.
I am also me, you are also you, and you are also me.
Sweetheart, I am in love with you so very much,
I am confused if I am you or you are me.

ney man manam o, nay to to'ii, ney to mani
ham man manam o, ham to to'ii, ham to mani
man bâ to chonânam, ey negâr-e khotani*
kan'dar ghalatam, ke man to'am ya to mani

*negâr-e khotani (translated here as "sweetheart") literally means "a beautiful
lady from Khotan," a town in Central Asia famous for its beautiful women.

36
When you look outward, you see the human forms.
You see strange people from West and East.
God said, "Return to me." How do you return?
Look inward: You will see beyond the human forms.

biiruun negari, suurat-e ensân biinii
khalği ajab az Ruum o Khorâsân biinii
farmuud ke arje'ii, rojuu' in bâshad?
bengar be daruun ke be-joz ensân biinii

(4)

THE BELOVED'S FACE

37

O Friend! I am your intimate companion.
Wherever you put your step, I am the soil beneath your foot.
In the religion of love, is this fair?
I see the whole world through you, but I can't see you.

> *ey duust be duusti ġariiniin torâ*
> *har jâ ke ġadam nehi, zamiiniim torâ*
> *dar maz'hab-e âsheġi ravâ key bâshad*
> *âlam be to biiniim o nabiiniim torâ?*

38

They ask me: "How come this pain,
this crying, sighing, and the pale face you have?"
"Don't ask," I say, "Questioning is not right.
If you see her beauty, it is so hard to take your eye off her."

> *guuyand marâ ke: in hame dard cherâst?*
> *vin naa'r-e vo âh o in rokh-e zard cherâst?*
> *goftam ke: chonin maguu, ke in kâr khatâst*
> *ruuy-e mahash bebiin o mosh'kel barkhâst*

39

Suddenly my sweetheart appeared through the door;
drinking from a glass of red wine, she sat by my side.
Watching and holding the charming curls of her long hair,
my whole face became an eye, and my two eyes became hands.

nâ'gah ze daram dar-âmad ân delbar-e mast
jâm-e mey-e laal nuush karde beneshast
az diidan o az gereftan-e zolf-e cho shast
ruuyam hame chashm gasht o chashmam hame dast

40

Every day, my sweetheart appears in a new fashion;
holding a cup, full of restless passion.
If I take it, the jug of my mind will crack.
If I don't accept, all day she will pull me back.

har ruuz be-no bar-âyad in delbar-e mast
ba sâghar-e por-fetne-ye por-shuur, be-dast
gar bestânam, ğarâbe-ye ağl shekast
var nastânam, nadânam az dastash rast

41

The sun of your face shines from beyond this sky.
To describe your beauty is beyond any language.
My love for you lies within my heart.
It is a mystery beyond this life, beyond this world.

khorshiid-e rokhat ze âsemân biirunast
chun hosn-e to kaz shar'h-e zabân biirunast
eshğ-e to daruun-e jân-e man jâ dârad
vin torfe ke az jân o jahân biirunast

42

As long as the face of that enviable angel is imprinted in my heart,
in the whole world, who is as joyous in heart as I?
O God, to live this happy life is all I know.
I keep hearing about sorrow; what it is, I don't know.

> *tâ dar del-e man suurat-e ân rashk pariist*
> *delshâd cho man, dar in hame âlam kiist?*
> *vallah ke be-joz shâd nemidânam ziist*
> *gham mishenavam, vali nemidânam chiist*

43

When the beloved rests in my bosom,
it is like having two thousand hearts in one body,
or the entire harvest contained in a grain of wheat
and a hundred worlds gathered in a needle's eye.

> *in torfe ke yâr dar dâman gonjad*
> *jân-e do hezâr tan dar-in tan gonjad*
> *dar yek gandom hezâr kharman gonjad*
> *sad âlam dar cheshme-ye suuzan gonjad*

44

You say, "In beauty, she is like the shining moon."
    Wrong! What is the moon before her?
You say, "In majesty, he is like a king."
    Wrong! What is the king before him?
Don't keep scolding me, "You get up so late!"
I have the sunshine in my bosom:
    How can I ever be late to rise at sunrise?

> *mâhash gofti, ghalat maguu, mah che bovad?*
> *shâhash gofti, khatâst ham, shah che bovad?*
> *tâ key guuyii marâ ke: bi-gah' khiizii?*
> *khorshiid cho ba man-ast, bi-gah' che bovad?*

45

Whoever sees you and does not smile in joy
or does not say "Wow" with an immense sense of wonder,
is what he is. His joy and wonder shall not increase.
He is good for no more than bricks and mortar for a prison wall.

ân kas ke to râ biinad o khandân nashavad
vaz heyrat-e to, goshâde dandân nashavad
chandân ke bovad, hezâr chandân nashavad
joz kâh'gel o kolukh-e zendân nashavad

46

Sometimes I call you my wine, sometimes my cup;
sometimes pure gold, sometimes silvery stone;
sometimes my bait, my trap or my prey.
All these I call you because I like to keep your name in silence.

gah' bâde lagab dâdam o gah' jâmash
gâhi zar-e pokhte, gâh' siim-e khâmash
gah' dâne vo gâh' seyd o gâhi dâmash
in jomle cherâst? tâ naguuyam nâmash

47

When I desire my heart, I know it is in your house.
When I desire my soul, I look at your hair.
When I drink water with such intense thirst,
I see your graceful face on water.

gar del talabam, bar sar-e kuuyat biinam
var jân talabam, bar sar-e muuyat biinam
az ghâyat-e tesh'negi agar âb khoram
dar âb hame khiyâl ruuyat biinam

48

My beloved and I were walking in a rose garden.
I gazed at a rose, unknowingly.
My sweetheart said, "Shame on you!
My face is here with you; yet you look at flowers!"

bâ yâr be golzâr shodam, rah'gozari
bar gol nazari fekandam, az bi-khabari
del'dâr be man goft ke: sharmat bâd
rokhsâr-e man injâ vo to dar gol negari?

(5)

DIE TO YOURSELF

49

At first, He pampered me with a thousand graces.
In the end, He burned me with a thousand griefs.
He played me like His favorite bead.
When I melted and became Him, He dropped me from the play.

avval be hezâr lotf be'navâkht marâ
akher be hezâr ghosse be'godâkht marâ
chon mohre-ye mehr-e khiish mi'bâkht marâ
chon man hame uu shodam, bar andâkht marâ

50

The hand of time shall silence this chattering noise.
The wolf of annihilation shall tear apart this wobbling flock.
In each person's head there is so much arrogance.
The flood of death shall hit from behind and wash it all away.

kuutâh konad zamâne in dam'dame râ
vaz ham bedarad gorg-e fanâ in rame râ
andar sar-e har kasi ghoruurist, valik
seyliyye ajal ǵafâ zanad in hame râ

51

When I die, take my corpse,
and surrender it to my Beloved.
If He kisses my decaying lips,
and I come back to life, do not marvel!

gar man bemram, marâ biyârid shomâ
morde be negâr-e man sepârid shomâ
gar buuse dahad bar lab-e puuside-ye man
gar zende shavam, ajab madârid shomâ

52

If you want your soul to be nourished and fulfilled;
        don't go to sleep.
Let the loving fire of the Beloved burn you;
        don't go to sleep.
For hundreds of nights you have slept; you know the outcome.
Do yourself a Divine favor: Tonight until dawn
        don't go to sleep.

gar miikhâhi baĝâ vo piruuz, makhosp
az âtash-e eshĝ-e duust, misuuz, makhosp
sad shab khofti o hâsel-e ân düdii
az bahr-e khodâ emshab tâ ruuz makhosp

53

Be fair! Love works for what is good.
It is the wicked character that causes harm.
You have given the name of love to your lust.
An enormous distance lies between love and lust.

ensâf bede, ke eshĝ niiku-kâr ast
zânast khelal ke tab' bad kerdâr ast
to shah'vat-e khüsh râ laĝab-e eshĝ nehi
az shah'vat tâ eshĝ rah besiyâr ast

54

I come from the Soul of souls, from the Life of lives.
I come from a town where homeless people live.
The road to that town is endless if you go with your legs and head.
Lose them; then you will have the real legs and head to go there.

man zân jânam ke jân'hâ râ jân ast
man zân shah'ram ke shahr-e bi'shah'rân ast
râh-e ân shahr râh-e bi'pâyân ast
ro bi sar o bi pâ sho, ke sar o pây ân ast

55

The secret of madness is the wellspring of wisdom.
Love's madman is also a man of refined knowledge.
One who becomes the heart's friend through the path of pain,
becomes a stranger to himself in a thousand ways.

sar'mây-ye aĝl, serre diivânegist
diivâne-ye eshĝ, mard-e farzânegist
ân kas ke shod ashenâ-ye del dar rah-e dard
ba khiishtanash hezâr biiganegist

56

I have this stubborn, careless, and nosy character,
and this sweetheart who is sensitive, impatient, and easily-bored.
Only God can come between the two of us:
A messenger from me to her, and vice versa.

jâni dâram lajuuj o sarmast o fozuul
vân'gah, yâri nâzok o bi'sabr o maluul
az man suuye yâr-e man rasul ast khodây
vaz yâr besuu-ye man khodây-ast rasul

57

I am a grape, rolling under the Beloved's crushing feet.
I roll in whatever direction love pulls and pushes me.
You say, "Why are you whirling around me?"
"I am not. I am whirling around myself which is you."

aguuram o dar ziir-e lagad mi'gardam
har suuy ke eshģ mi'keshad, mi'gardam
gofti ke: be-gerd-e man cherâ mi'gardii
gerd-e to niyam, be-gerd-e khod mi'gardam

58

Today I shall go out for a long, languishing walk.
I shall make my skull a jar and offer wine from it.
Drunken, I shall walk in the town
to find a wise man and make him drunk and insane.

emruuz yeki gardesh-e mastâne konam
vaz kâse-ye sar, sâghar o peymâne konam
emruuz dar in shahr hami gardam mast
mijuuyam âģeli, ke divâne konam

59

So full of yourself, you cannot taste drunkenness;
attached to your Flesh, you cannot be devoted to the Soul.
In the path of love, you will not reach the real being
until you let go of yourself like water and fire.

tâ hosh'yâri, be taa'me masti naresi
tâ tan nadahi, be jân parasti naresi
tâ dar rah-e eshģ-e duust chon âtash o âb
az khod nashavi niist, be hasti naresi

60

Your *self* is a snake in the day and a fish at night.
Look carefully, which one of these is your life companion?
Sometimes you sit with Harut* the Sorcerer in a dark well.
Sometimes you abide in the heart of Venus,
          watching over your beautiful moon.

> *jân ruuz cho mâr ast o be shab chon mâhi*
> *bengar ke to bâ kodâm jân ham'râhi*
> *gah bâ Hâruut-e sâher andar châhi*
> *gah dar del-e Zoh're, pâseban-e mâhi*

*According to a legend in the Quran, Harut and Marut were two angels sent by God to test the faith of the Babylonians, but they became sorcerers, and were, therefore, sentenced to a life in a dark well.

(6)

THE ART OF LIVING

61

Love is my only real companion
from the beginning to the end of life.
From deep inside me, the soul cries out:
Oh, lazy one on the path of love, open the heart and set me free.

joz eshĝ nabud hiich damsâz marâ
ney avval o ney âkher o âghâz marâ
jân mi'dahad az daruune, âvâz marâ
key kâhel-e râh-e eshĝ, dar bâz marâ

62

We are lovers of love.
    Submission to a creed is something else.
We are poor ants, collecting love.
    Solomon's kingly life is something else.
In our longing, we have pale faces and torn hearts to offer.
If you desire a fashion market, go somewhere else.

mâ asheĝ-e eshĝiim o mosalmân degar ast
mâ muur-e za'iifiim o Soleymân degar ast
az mâ rokh-e zard o jegar-e pâre talab
bâzârche-ye ĝasab foruushân degar ast

63

Walk on the spiritual path, even though it is never-ending.
Watching at a distance is not bravery.
You can master this path by living in your heart.
The life of the flesh is just animal lust.

> *dar neh ğadam, arche râh bi'pâyân-ast*
> *kaz duur nazzârr-e kardan kâr-e na'mardân-ast*
> *in râh, ze zendegi-ye del hâsel kon*
> *kin zendegi-ye tan, sefat-e heyvân-ast*

64

Whenever my heart searches for words to describe you,
I know it will soon end up in shame!
Your beauty should be in my remembrance for so long
that your image appears in every breath.

> *ânjâ ke bahr-e sokhan del-e mâ gardad*
> *man mi'dânam ke zuud rosvâ gardad*
> *chandân bekonad yâd-e jamâl-e khosh-e to*
> *kaz har nafasash naĝsh-e to peydâ gardad*

65

In love, there are no lower or higher positions,
neither stupidity nor cleverness,
no preachers, masters or disciples, either.
Love is the freedom of spirit – humbleness and bravery together.

> *dar eshĝ, na pastii na bolandi bâshad*
> *ney bi'huushii, ney huushmandi bâshad*
> *ĝorrâ-yii o sheykhi-yo moriidi na-bovad*
> *ĝallâshi-yo kam zani-yo rendi bâshad*

66

Keep the company of lovers only.
Don't even think of mingling with mean people.
Every group calls you to itself. Be careful!
The crow leads you to the ruins; the parrot to sweet home.

joz soh'bat-e âshegan o mastân mapasand
dar del havas-e go'm-e forumâye maband
har tây'fe-at be jâneb-e khiish keshand
zâgh-at suuy-e viirâne vo tuuti suuy-e gand

67

Be diligent like a falcon; be majestic like a leopard:
Victorious in the fight, elegant in hunting.
Spend less time with the nightingale and the peacock:
One ruins your sleep at night; the other is just color in daylight.

bâ hemmat-e bâz bâsh o bâ kebr-e palang
ziibâ be gah-e shekâr o piruuz be jang
kam kon bar-e andalib o tâvuus derang
kânjâ hame âfat ast o injâ hame rang

68

One day I was drinking wine at your tavern,
cleansing this robe of mud, refreshing the soul.
Suddenly I saw this well-built universe through that ruined tavern.
Hence, I dance whether I feel ruined or well-built.

ruuzi be kharâbat-e to, mey mi'khordam
in kharge-ye âb o gel, bedar mi'kardam
diidam ze kharâbat-e to âlam maa'muur
maa'muur o kharâb az an chonin mi'gardam

69

I say to myself: Don't keep the company of sorrowful, negative people;
be with those who have joyous hearts and sweet tongues.
You come to the garden not to touch thorns;
but spend time with the rose, jasmine, and jonquil.

goftam ke: bar-e hariif-e ghamgin maneshin
joz pah'lu-ye khosh delân-e shiiriin maneshin
dar bâgh dar-âmadi, suu-ye khâr maro
joz bâ gol o yâsaman o nasriin maneshin

70

My restless heart journeyed all over the world
to find the water of life to cure me.
In the end that sweet water
burst out from the granite of my own heart.

bar gerd-e jahân, in del-e âvâre-ye man
besiyâr safar kard, pey-e châre-ye man
vân âb-e hayât-e khosh o khosh khâre-ye man
juushiid o bar-âmad ze del-e khâre-ye man

71

Childhood passed, so did youth.
Old age came on the wing of life.
A guest stays for no more than three days.
O guest of this world, if your three days have passed,
        ride your little donkey higher than the mundane field.

shod kuudaki-yo raft javâni ze javân
ruuz-e piirii rasid, bar par ze jahân
har meh'mân râ se ruuz bâshad peymân
ey khâje, se ruuz shod, kharak bartar rân

72

Do good things; the world appreciates goodness.
And goodness cannot be taken away from you.
Everyone's wealth is left here, so will be yours.
Better to leave your goodness than the perishable wealth.

ro niikii kon, ke dahr niikii dânad
uu niikii râ ze nikovân nastânad
mâl az hame mânad o az to ham khâhad mând
ân beh' ke be jây-e mâl, niikii mânad

(7)

NIGHT SECRETS

73

It is late night and we are alone, lost in love
on a sea with no shore in sight.
The boat, the night, the clouds, and we
are all sailing on the Sea of God and by His grace.

afsuus ke bügâh shod o mâ sheydâ (tanhâ)
dar daryâ-yii, kanâre-ash nâ-peydâ
kashti o shab o ghammâm o mâ mi'râniim
dar bahr-e khodâ, be fazl o tofiĝ-e khodâ

74

My Friend! If you don't see me in your dream tonight,
you won't see me for another year, either.
O, Night! Whenever you look at me
you won't see me without the morning light by my side.

ey khâje, be khâb dar, nabiinii mâ râ
ta sâl-e degar, degar nabiinii mâ râ
ey shab, har dam ke jâneb-e mâ negari
bi roshani-ye sahar nabiinii mâ râ

75

When I am with you, I can't sleep because of our intense love.
When you are not with me, I can't go to sleep because of my lament.
Praise to God! I stay awake both nights,
but see the difference between that and this wakefulness.

tâ bâ to bovam, nakhos'pam az yârii'hâ
tâ bi to bovam, nakhos'pam az zârii'hâ
sob'hân allâh, ke har do shab büdâram
to farġ negar miyân-e biidârii'hâ

76

My beloved, tonight be like the shining moon.
     Don't go to sleep.
Let's whirl and dance, like the heavens above us.
     Don't go to sleep.
Our wakefulness is a lamp onto the world.
Tonight, let's hold up this lamp.
     Don't go to sleep.

ey mâh, chonin shabi, to mah'vâr, makhosp
dar door dar â, cho charkh-e davvâr, makhosp
bidâri-ye mâ cherâġh-e âlam bâshad
yek shab to cherâġh râ negah'dâr, makhosp

77

One who is not aware of Him is asleep.
One who becomes aware cannot sleep.
Every night, love whispers to my eyes:
"Woe to the one who goes to sleep without Him."

ân sar ke bovad bi-khabar az vey, khospad
ân kas ke khabar yâft az uu, key khospad?
mi'guuyad eshġ dar do cheshmam hame shab:
vây bar ân kasi ke bi-vey khospad

78

Last night, my beloved was like the shining moon in the sky.
No, she was even more beautiful than sunshine.
Her beauty is just outside the circle of my imagination.
I only know she is nice and graceful; I don't know how or why.

duush ân bot-e man, ham'cho mah-e garduun bud
ney, ney, ke be-hosn, az aftâb afzuun bud
az dâyere-ye khyâl-e mâ biriuun bud
dânam ke neku bud, nadânam chuun bud

79

The night passed. Where did it go? Where it was before.
Every creature goes back home.
O Night, when you reach the Promised Land,
tell the Beloved how I am.

shab raft, kojâ raft? hamân jây ke bud
tâ khâne ravad bâz yagin har mojud
ey shab, cho ravi bedân magâm-e mo'ud
az man berasân ke ân felâni chuun bud

80

I am not insane, but that is what they call me.
I am not a stranger, but like a stranger they banish me.
Like guardsmen who come out at midnight.
They are drunk; yet they see me as if in daylight.

divâne niyam, va lik mi'khanan'dam
bigâne niyam, va lik mi'rânan'dam
ham'chon assân be jahad dar nim-shabân
mastand, vali cho ruuz mi'dânan'dam

81

Last night my beloved visited me so graciously.
I said to the Night, "Don't reveal this secret tomorrow."
The Night said, "Look well! The sunshine is with you.
How can I even break to daylight?"

> *duush âmade bud az sar-e lotfi, yâram*
> *shab râ goftam: fâsh makon asrâram*
> *shab goft: pas o piish negah' kon âkhar*
> *khorshiid to dâri, ze kojâ sob'h bar âram?*

82

Do you know what night time is for? Night is
for lovers to be together, away from strangers.
Like this special night: My beautiful beloved is in the house with me.
I am drunk; she is in love; and the night goes crazy.

> *dâni shab chiist? beshno ey farzâne*
> *khalvat kon-e âshegân ze har beigâne*
> *khasse emshab, ke hast mah ham-khâne*
> *man mastam o mah âsheg o shab divâne*

* "My beautiful beloved" is a metaphorical translation of the "moon" (*mah*).

83

Last night, you treated me so graciously.
This morning you have thrown me back, like your long hair.
Your eyes are drunk with you,
          and mine drunk with looking at your eyes.
You can't attend to your own drunken eyes;
          how can you care for mine?

> *lotfi ke marâ shabâne benavâkh'te'ii*
> *emruuz cho zolf-e khod, pas andâkh'te'ii*
> *chashm-e to ze to mast o man az chashm'e to mast*
> *zân mast bedin mast, napardâkh'te'ii*

84

Last night, in a dream, I saw a beautiful face
  standing by the door, shining like the moon,
graceful, like the sea; full of wonders and splendor.
Today, I go door to door, inquiring.
Perhaps someone would recognize that lovely face from my dream.

man duush be khâb dar bedidam ġamari
daryâ sefati, ajâyebi, siimbari
emruuz be gerde har dari migardam
kaz yârak-e duushine ke dârad khabari

(8)

WATER OF LIFE

85

One life passes; God gives another life.
After *fanâ* (death of the ego) you shall see *baġâ* (real life).
Love is the Water of Life. Enter this water:
Each droplet contains a sea of life.

> *gar omr beshod, omr-e degar dâd khodâ*
> *gar omr-e fanâ namând, nek omr-e baġâ*
> *eshġ âb-e hayâtast, dar in âb darâ*
> *har ġatre az in, bahr-e hayâtist jodâ*

86

The one who has taken sleep away from me,
now wishes my sanctuary be watered with my tears.
Silently, He seized me and threw me into that water,
and it sweetened the bitter water in me.

> *ân kas ke bebaste ast uu khâb-e marâ*
> *tar mi'khâhad ze ashk, meh'râb-e marâ*
> *khamush marâ gereft o dar âb afkand*
> *âbi ke halâvati dahad âb-e marâ*

87

You have a heart as vast as the sea. Be brave!
Give away gems and jewels. Misers cannot journey this path.
Your body is like a seashell. Its open mouth cries: "So small I am.
How could I contain sea treasures
          if the spirit had not found its way into me?"

ey daryâ del, to gohar o marjân râ
dar bâz, ke râh niist kam-kharjân râ
tan hamchon sadaf, dahân goshâdast ke âh
man key gonjam cho rah nashod mar jân râ?

88

To the boat passing on the sea,
reeds on the shore appear to be passing by.
Likewise, we pass by and depart this life,
thinking that the world is passing by.

kashti ke be daryâ-ye ravân mi'gozarad
mi'pendârad ke neyestân mi'gozarad
mâ mi'gozarim zin jahân dar reh'lat
mi'pendârim kin jahân mi'gozarad

89

You seek pearl, but the little stream yields no pearl.
The pearl seeker must dive into the depth of the sea.
And one who emerges from the Water of Life thirsty
deserves to have that precious gem.

dorr mitalabi, ze cheshme dorr bar-nâyad
juuyande-ye dorr be ġaar-e daryâ bâyad
in gohar-e ġeymati kasi râ shâyad
kaz âb-e hayât teshne beruun âyad

90

He has come. The one who had never left us is here.
He is water, and the stream is never empty.
He is the mine of musk; we are its scent.
Have you ever seen musk apart from its scent?

âmad âmad, ânk-e naraft uu hargez
khâli nabod ân âb azin juu hargez
uu maa'dan-e moshk o mâ hame buuye ve-yiim
az moshk jodâ to diide-ii buu hargez?

91

The whole world is brimming with Jesus' breath:
How can the world contain even the robe of Anti-Christ?
How can the bitter water of a dark soul remain
in an ocean filled with pure and pleasant water?

por az isiist in jahân mâlâ'mâl
key gonjad dar jahân, gomâsh'e dajjâl?
shuurâbe-ye talkh-e tiire del key gonjad
chon moshk jahân porast az âb-e zolâl?

92

I once drank water from the sweet stream of the Friend.
I was refreshed, delighted, sweetened.
In that ecstasy, I have become a waterwheel,
turning and turning as the Water of Life flows.

az juuye khosh âb-e duust âbii khordam
khosh kardam o khosh khordam o khosh âvardam
khod râ bar juush, âsiyâ-yii kardam
tâ âb-e hayât mi'ravad, mi'gardam

93

Rise! Let's take the moonlight to the night garden;
and shake the sleep off the rose and narcissus.
For months our ship has been sliding on ice;
it's time, my friends, to sail on the sea water.

khiiziid, ke tâ bar shab mah'tab zaniim
bar bâgh-e gol o narges bi-khâb zaniim
kashti se mâh bar sar-e yakh râldiim
vağtast barâdarân, ke bar âb zaniim

94

We are hidden treasures in clay forms.
We are owners of the eternal land.
When we pass the darkness of this muddy water,
we are both the water of life and the guide* to it.

dar âlam-e gel, ganj-e nahâni, mâyiim
dârande-ye molk-e jâvedâni, mâyiim
chon az zolomât-e âb o gel bogzashtiim
ham khezr o ham âb-e zendegâni, mâyiim

* "Guide to the Water of Life" is the legendary sage Khezr in Sufi literature.

95

Love is this: The hidden alchemy of the East,
and the cloud carrying a hundred thousand lightnings within.
Deep inside me flows the ocean of the Beloved's splendor,
carrying the entire cosmos within.

eshğ ast ke kimiyâ-ye sharğ ast daruu
abriist ke sad hezâr barğ ast daruu
dar bâten man ze farre uu daryâ-yiist
kin jomle-ye kâyenat ğharğ ast daruu

96

In this tent we live, we are prisoners.
Outside these veils, we are free and our own masters.
The Water of Life says to people,
"Leave your dead self on the shore, and then enter."

har chand dar in parde asiriid hame
zin parde beruun raviid, amiriid hame
ân âb-e hayât, khalg ra mi'guuyad:
bar sâhel-e juuy-e mâ bemiriid hame

(9)

FIRE OF LOVE

97

The fire of love bakes me in the day.
It drags me to the tavern every night.
It makes me sit with the tavern folks.
Other people don't recognize me anymore.

> *in âtash-e eshq mi'pazânad mâ râ*
> *har shab be kharâbât mi'keshânad mâ râ*
> *bâ ahl-e kharâbat neshânad mâ râ*
> *tâ gheyr-e kharâbât nadânad mâ râ*

98

Love is the path of our Prophet.
We were born from love, our Mother.
Alas! Our Mother is concealed within our veils,
hidden from our denying, ignoring character.

> *eshġ ast tariġ o râh-e peyghâmbar-e mâ*
> *mâ zâde-ye eshġ o eshġ bod mâdar-e mâ*
> *ey mâdar-e mâ, nehofte dar châdor-e mâ*
> *pen'hân shode az tabii'at-e kâfer-e mâ*

99

If no fire is burning in the heart, how come this smoke?
If no incense is burning in the world, how come this smell?
Here I am. How can you say a good lover is a dead lover?
The moth burns in the candle's flame, but it is happy. Why?

gar âtash-e del niist, pas in duud cherâst?
var uud nasuukht, buuy-e in uud cherâst?
in buudan-e man âsheg-e nâbuud cherâst?
parvâne ze suuz-e sham' khoshnuud cherâst?

100

In the gathering of lovers the rules are otherwise.
The wine of love is sold in a different liquor store.
The knowledge you gained in school
is one thing; love is otherwise.

dar majles-e osh'shâq garârii degar ast
in bâde-ye eshg râ khammârii degar ast
ân elm ke dar madrase hâsel kardand
kârii degar ast o eshg kârii degar ast

101

Our Judge is not like the other judges.
He is not a pair of scissors; he doesn't cut the precious silk into pieces.
He has been a Lover since the dawn of eternity.
Only a ruling of love can satisfy Him.

ân gazi-ye mâ, cho digarân gazi niist
meylash be suuy-e atlas o megrâzi niist
shod gâzi-ye mâ âsheg az ruuz-e azal
bâ gheyr-e gazây-e eshg, uu râzi niist

102

Love is what gives joy to creatures.
Love is what provides all sorts of happiness.
We were not born from women; love gave birth to us.
A hundred blessings and praises to our mothers!

eshĝ ân bâshad ke khalĝ râ dârad shâd
eshĝ ân bâshad ke dâd-e shâdi-hâ dâd
mâ râ mâdar nazâd, ân eshĝ bezâd
sad rah'mat o afariin bar-ân mâdar bâd

103

Love comes from beginningless time and will go on for eternity,
and countless will be the seekers of love.
Tomorrow, on the day of reckoning,
whoever is not in love will fail.

eshĝ az azalast o tâ be abad khâhad bud
juuyande-ye eshĝ bi-adad khâhad bud
fardâ ke ĝiyâmat âshekârâ gardad
ey har ki na âsheĝ ast radd khâhad bud

104

This day is for singing, listening, dancing.
This day is bright, prosperous in the rays of light.
This love is one whole given to all.
This love is a kiss of death to the calculating reason.

emruuz samâ' ast o samâ' ast o samâ'
nuur ast o shoâ' ast o shoâ' ast o shoâ'
in eshĝ masha' ast o masha' ast o masha'
az aĝl vedâ' ast o vedâ' ast o vedâ'

105

This wine renders the power of flight to the bird soul,
and frees our life and soul from weariness and depression.
This love is served by a beautiful cupbearer;
        that is why all lovers are drunk.
This wine is allowed in the religion of love. Lovers, cheers!

an mey ke goshuud morgh-e jân râ par o bâl
jân râ berahânüd ze sürri-yo malâl
saği eshğ ast o âsheğân mâlâ'mâl
az eshğ pazürofte vo bar mâst halâl

106

This love is perfect, perfecting, perfection.
This ego is fantasy, fantasizing, fantasized.
This light of consciousness is glory, glorifying, glorified.
This day is for union, unifying, unity.

in eshğ kamâl ast o kamâl ast o kamâl
in nafs khayâl ast o khayâl ast o khayâl
in nuur jalâl ast o jalâl ast o jalâl
emruuz vesâl ast o vesâl ast o vesâl

107

My heart, it is time I turn my attention to you.
Out of your corals, I shall make a fire temple.
You are a gold mine hidden in my life.
To reveal your brilliance I should throw you into the fire of love.

ân vağt âmad ke mâ be to pardâzüm
marjân-e to râ khâne-ye âtash sâzüm
to kân zarrü, miyân-e jânü pen'hân
tâ sâf shavü, dar âtashat andâzüm

108

I am in love with love; and love with me.
The body is here to love the soul; the soul to love the body.
Sometimes I put my arms around the beloved's neck.
Sometimes he gently pulls me by my robe, like lovers do.

man âsheg-e eshg o eshg ham âsheg-e man
tan âsheg-e jân âmad o jân âsheg-e tan
gah' man âram do dast andar gardan
gah' uu keshadam cho del'robâyân, dâman

(10)

UNITY AND UNION

109

The day my essence joins the all-pervading ocean
all of my particles shall shine in their splendor.
On the path of love, I burn like a candle
so that all moments of my life merge in a single moment.

ân vaĝt ke bahr-e koll shavad zât marâ
roshan gardad jamâl-e zarrât marâ
zan misuuzam cho sham', tâ dar rah-e eshĝ
yek vaĝt shavad jomle-ye oĝât marâ

110

Riding on the horse of love we have come here from Emptiness.
Our night is bright as we drink from the wine of union.
This special wine is allowed in the religion of lovers.
You will not see our lips dry until we depart at the dawn of Emptiness.

bâ eshĝ ravân shodam az adam markab-e mâ
roshan ze sharâb-e vasl dâ'em shab-e mâ
zân mey ke harâm nüst dar maz'hab-e mâ
tâ sob'h-e adam khoshk nayâbi lab-e mâ

111

Wherever I put my head down, I prostrate to Him.
In all directions of the earth and beyond I worship Him.
The garden, roses, parrots, music, dance, and lovely faces
all are excuses and means. He is the real end.

> *bar har jâyii ke sar neham, masjuud uust*
> *dar shesh jahat o beruun-e shesh, maa'buud uust*
> *bâgh o gol o bolbol o samâ' o shâhed*
> *in jomle bahâne ast, magsuud uust*

112

He is the inside and the outside of my heart.
The life pulse, blood and veins of my body are all He.
How can belief or unbelief be contained in me?
Since He is all in all, there is no other being like me.

> *andar del-e man daruun or biiruun hame uust*
> *andar tan-e man jân o rag o khuun hame uust*
> *injây cheguune kofr o iimân gonjad?*
> *bi-chun bâshad vojuud-e man, chon hame uust*

113

You are ignorant of your own mind and deceived by your skin.
Awake! There is a Friend in your life, within you.
Your brain senses the body,
        but the core of your consciousness is the soul.
When you go beyond the body, the senses and the soul,
        He is all in all.

> *ey bi-khabar az maghz, shode ghorre be puust*
> *hosh dâr, ke dar miyân-e jân, dârii duust*
> *hess maghz-e tan-ast o maghz-e hessat jânat*
> *chon az tan o hess o jân gozashtii, hame uust*

114

The Water of Life comes from the Beloved. It heals every illness.
In the rose-garden of His union, no bitter thorn remains.
They say, "There is a window between hearts."
How can there be a window? No wall remains between us.

az âb-e hayât-e duust biimâr namând
vaz golbon-e vasl-e duust yek khâr namând
guuyand: dariche-iist az del suuy-e del
che jây-e dariche? ke diivâr namând

115

In the house of the Beloved, lovers come to be nourished, and then go.
In His presence, they wash away their tears of blood, and then go.
I am like the soil on the doorway of the Beloved's house.
I wish to stay. The others are like the wind; they come and go.

dar kuuy-e to, âshegân fazâyand o ravand
khuun-e jegar az diide goshâyand o ravand
man bar dar-e to mogim bâdâm, cho khâk
var'ney degarân cho bâd âyand o ravand

116

Until selfishness completely dies in a person,
his heart will not realize union and oneness.
Oneness is not imported from the outside;
        union means "you" is naught.
Worthless words, no matter how many,
        cannot turn illusion into truth.

tâ bande ze khod fâni-ye motlag nashavad
tohiid be nazd-e uu mohaggag nashavad
tohiid holuul niist, nâ-buudan-e tost
var'ney be gazâf bâteli hagg nashavad

117

In the path of spiritual quest, one must first become ripe
and then detached from worldly life.
One must also correct his eyesight because although
He is in the whole world, a discerning eye is required to see Him.

> *dar râh-e talab, rasiide-yii mibâyad*
> *dâman ze jahân kashide-yii mibâyad*
> *binâyi-ye khüsh râ davâ kon, var'ney*
> *âlam hame uust, diide-yii mibâyad*

118

In the sea of serenity and purity, I dissolved like salt.
Belief, unbelief, conviction, doubt – none remained.
A star appeared inside my heart.
The seven heavens disappeared in that star's light.

> *dar bahr-e safâ godâkhtam ham'cho namak*
> *ney kofr o ney iimân, na yagin mând na shakk*
> *andar del-e man, setâre-yii peydâ shod*
> *gom gasht dar ân setâre, har haft falak*

119

We are the mirror, also the face in it.
Drunk from eternal wine, we are also the cup we sip from.
We prevent illness; we also cure it.
We are the water of life, also the jar that pours it.

> *ham âyine-yim, ham legâ-yim hame*
> *sar-mast piyâle-ye baga-yim hame*
> *ham dâfe-e ranj, va ham shafâ-yim hame*
> *ham âb-e hayât, ham saggâ-yim hame*

120

You are Water; we are plants.
You are the King; we are beggars.
You are the Speaker; we are the sounds.
You are the Seeker; why should we all not be the finders?

to âbi, va mâ jomle giyâ-yim hame
to shâhi, va mâ jomle gedâ-yim hame
guuyande to-yii, va ma sadâ-yim hame
juuyande to-yii, chera nayâbim hame

(11)

PEACEFUL MIND

121

Watch out, my heart! Don't let sorrows come in.
Even for the whole world,
          don't engage with the strangers to the heart.
Since you are content with a little bread and vegetables,
don't value the world's vanities more than that.

> *zenhâr delâ, be khod made rah, gham râ*
> *magozin be jahân, soh'bat-e nâ-mahram râ*
>   *ba tarre vo nâni cho ganâ'at kardi*
>   *chon tarre masanj, sablat-e âlam râ*

122

The One who fashioned your one and only image
will not abandon you in your imaginings.
In the image field of your heart,
He will raise hundreds of beautiful friends.

> *ân kas ke to râ nagsh konad uu tan'hâ*
> *tan'hâ nagozâ'radat miyân-e sodâ*
>   *dar khâne-ye tasviir-e to, yaani del-e to*
>   *bar ruuyânad do sad hariif-e ziibâ*

123

Peaceful is the one
    who is not concerned with having more or less;
    is not attached to being a sultan or a dervish;
    is free from worldly sorrows and worldly people;
    and is not attached, even for a bit, to himself.

asuude kasi ke dar kamo büishii niist
dar band-e tavângari yo darviishii niist
fâregh ze gham-e jahân o az khalg-e jahân
bâ khüsh'tanash be zarre-yii khüshii niist

124

Beyond our "denying" and "submitting," there is a vast plain.
How I wish we could meet there.
When the mystic arrives there, (s)he lies down to relax.
Belief or unbelief has no place there.

az kofr o az islâm beruun, sahrâ-yist
mâ râ be miyân-e ân fazâ, sodâ-yist
âref cho bedân rasiid, sar râ benehad
ney kofr o na islâm, na ânjâ jâ-yist

125

All our sufferings arise from our foolish greed,
from the lustful ego, and from our itching for power and fame.
The bird that falls into the snare to eat a few grains,
falls from an open roof into a tight cage.

mâ râ hame ranj, az tamaa-e khâm oftâd
vaz shah'vat-e nafs o khâresh-e kâm oftâd
morghi ke barâye dâne dar dâm oftâd
andar gafas-e tang ze lab-e bâm oftâd

126

Do not let sorrow and suffering overwhelm you;
do not let worldly desires occupy the world of your heart.
Drink from the wine of love, day and night,
before the law of death consumes your mouth.

magozâr ke ghosse dar miyânat giirad
yâ vas'vase-hâ-ye in jahânat giirad
ro sharbat-e eshĝ dar dahân neh, shab or ruuz
zân piish ke hokm-e haĝĝ dahânat giirad

127

My sick heart, it's time for your medicine.
Take a deep refreshing breath! The time has come.
The Beloved, who heals the sick hearts of lovers,
has come to our world in a human form.

hân ey del-e khaste, vaĝt-e mar'ham âmad
khosh khosh nafasi bezan, ke ân dam âmad
yâri ke azuu kâr shavad yârân râ
dar suurat-e âdami, be âlam âmad

128

Do not grieve my heart! The one, who relieves hearts, has arrived.
He has come with powerful songs to comfort you.
The wings of your sorrows, small as flies, are soon to be broken,
for the Phoenix from the Heavenly Mountain has arrived.

deltang masho, ke delgoshâyii âmad
del-e nik navâz-e bâ navâyii âmad
gham râ cho magas, shekast aknun par o bâl
kaz jâneb-e ĝâf-e jân homâyii âmad

129

Without love, there is no real joy and delight.
Without love, life lacks beauty and harmony.
Hundreds of raindrops fall from the cloud into the sea.
But only the stirring power of love grows pearls in sea shells.*

> *bi eshǧ, neshât o tarab afzuun nashavad*
> *bi eshǧ, vojud khuub o mozuun nashavad*
> *sad ǧatre ze abr agar be daryâ bârad*
> *be jonbesh-e eshǧ, dorr-e maknuun nashavad*

* This line refers to the ancient, and now out-dated, idea that pearls grow
  from water drops trapped in sea shells.

130

The emptier your hands and hearts are, the better for you.
The freer the heart is, the more joyous it is, the better for you.
Being happy in spiritual poverty even for the twinkling of an eye
is far better than the majesty of a hundred thousand kings.

> *dast o del-e mâ, har'che tohii'tar, khosh'tar*
> *va âzadi-ye del, ze har'che khosh'tar, khosh'tar*
> *eysh-e khosh moflesâne, yek chashm zadan*
> *az hesh'mat-e sad hezâr ǧeysar, khosh'tar*

131

I say to myself: Do not put yourself above others.
Be like a caring drug, not the snake's poisonous fang.
Do you wish to be safe from the evil-doings of others?
Don't speak evil! Don't mingle with evil-doing people! Don't think evil!

> *bâ del goftm: ze diigarân, büsh ma'bâsh*
> *ro mar'ham-e lotf bâsh, chon niish ma'bâsh*
> *khâhi ke ze hich kas be to bad narasad*
> *bad guuy-o bad âmiiz o bad andiish ma'bâsh*

132

Here we are, rejoicing even without wine.
Every morning we wake up glowing;
      every evening we go to be bed gratified.
They say, "There is no future for you."
Here we are, rejoicing without the future!

> *mâyiim ke bi bâde vo bi jâm, khoshiim*
> *har sob'h monavvarim o har shâm khoshiim*
> *guuyand: sar'anjâm nadârüd shomâ*
> *mâyiim ke bi hich sar'anjâm khoshiim*

(12)

RUMI ON HIS LIFE, POETRY AND DEATH

133

Wherever in the world people plant seeds of friendship,
they bring those seeds from my farmland.
Wherever they play the flute and tambourine with such joy,
that is my joy; they think it is theirs.

har jâ be jahân tokhm-e vafâ mi'kârand
vân tokhm ze kharman'gah-e mâ mi'ârand
har jâ ze tarab nây o dafi bar dârand
ân shâdi-ye mâst, ân-e khod pendârand

134

The Sufi shares with you the secrets of inner life.
Each moment, he gives away a treasure land, for free.
The Sufi doesn't beg for your bread.
He begs to give life to you.

darviish ke asrâr-e nahân mi'bakh'shad
har dam molki be râyegân mi'bakh'shad
darviish kasi niist ke nân mi'talabad
darviish kasi bovad ke jân mi'bakh'shad

135

As the flames of your love engulfed my heart,
all that I had was burned to ashes; only your love remained.
I put my mind, learning, and books on the shelf;
and learned the art of poetry and singing.

> *tâ dar del-e man eshģ-e to afruukhte shod*
> *joz eshģ-e to har che dâshtam suukhte shod*
> *aģl-o sabģ-o ketâb bar tâģ nehâd*
> *she'r-o ghazal-o do-beyti âmuukhte shod*

136

When the power of contemplation gave life to my poetic talent,
the goddess of poetry occupied my mind and tongue.
A thousand lovely girls are displayed in my verses;
each pregnant, like the Virgin Mary.

> *tab'am cho hayât yâft az jelve-ye fekr*
> *âvard aruus-e nazm dar hojre-ye zekr*
> *dar har beyti hezâr dokhtar benomuud*
> *har yek be mesâl-e Maryam, âbestan o bekr*

137

I burned my shop, work and business.
Making poems and songs is my new skill.
I burned my own life, heart and eyes
for the love of Him, who is my life, heart and eyes.

> *mâ kâr o dokkân o püshe râ suukhte-üm*
> *she'r o ghazal o do-beyti âmuukhte-üm*
> *dar eshģ ke uu jân o del o diide-ye mâst*
> *jân o del o diide, har se râ suukhte-üm*

138

You were too quiet and shy; I made you a story teller.
You were a pious ascetic; I made you a singer of love songs.
In the world, you had no fame, no title;
I sat with you and made you a knower of the inner signs.

khâmuush bodi, fasâne guuyat kardam
zâhed bodi, tarâne guuyat kardam
andar âlam na nâm buudat na neshân
beneshân-damat, neshâne guuyat kardam

139

I learned the art of loving because of your perfection.
I owe my art of poetry to your beauty.
On the canvas of my heart, your image dances.
I learned the art of dancing because of your image.

man âshegi az kamâl-e to âmuuzam
beyt-o ghazal az jamâl-e to âmuuzam
dar parde-ye del, khayâl-e to rags konad
man rags ham az khayâl-e to âmuuzam

140

My poems and songs were washed away by water.
The flood took away even the clothes I didn't have yet!
My vice, virtue and piety were all gifts from the moonlight,
and the moonlight took them back.

beyt-o ghazal-o she'r-e mârâ âb bebord
rakhtii ke nadâshtiim, seylâb bebord
niik-o bad-o zohd-o pâr'sâyi-e mârâ
mahtâb bedâd o mahtâb bebord

141

I recited a verse, but my sweetheart became upset.
"Do you measure my beauty by the scale of this verse?" she said.
"You tell me what poem I recite for you," I pleaded.
"What poem can ever do justice to my presence?" she rightly said.

> *bar goftam beyt, delbar az man ranjiid*
> *goftâ ke be vazn-e beyt, mârâ sanjiid?*
> *goftam ke kodâm beyt guuyam, farmâ*
> *goftâ be kodâm beyt khâham gonjiid?*

142

My turban, robe and head, three put together
are worth less than a penny.
As for me: Haven't you heard my world-wide fame?
But, actually I am nobody, nobody, nobody.

> *dastâram-o jobbe-am-o saram, har se be ham*
> *geymat kardand be yek deram chiizii kam*
> *nashenidasti to nâm-e man dar âlam?*
> *man hich-kasam, hich-kasam, hich-kasam*

143

Whoever passes by my grave will become ecstatic.
If he stops to see my grave, he will be drunk all his life.
Then if he swims in the sea, all sea water and boats will dance in joy;
and when he dies and is buried, the soil of his grave will be drunk.

> *bar guur-e man ân ku gozarad, mast shavad*
> *var iist konad, tâ be abad mast shavad*
> *dar bahr ravad, bahr o amad mast shavad*
> *dar khâk ravad, guur or lahad mast shavad*

144

I am both secular and religious; I am both pure wine and dregs.
I am old, young, and also a little child.
When I die, don't say, "He died."
Say, "He was dead, he became alive, and his Friend took him away."

ham kofram-o ham diinam-o ham sâfi-ye dord
ham piiram-o ham javân-o ham kuudak-e khord
gar man bemram marâ maguuyiid ke mord
gu morde bod o zende shod o duust bebord

LAST POEM

145

Through love, all that is cold becomes warm-hearted.
In the light of love, hard stones soften and melt.
Do not be harsh to lovers for their abnormalities.
The wine of love has made them mad and impudent.

az âtash-e eshĝ, sard-hâ garm shavad
vaz tâbesh-e eshĝ, sang-hâ narm shavad
ey duust, gonâh-e âshegân sakht magiir
kaz bâde-ye eshĝ mard bi-sharm shavad

Part III

COMPASSION & WISDOM IN ACTION

12+1 Stories from Rumi's Life

"I think for Rumi joy is primary. To some people, the world is filled with grief, but Rumi would say, 'I think that the world is primarily graceful, a gift."

Coleman Barks in conversation with Bill Moyers
The Language of Life (PBS, 1995)

"The heart of the spiritual life, the enduring substance of the journey, is the refinement of our own inner landscape – humility, egolessness, selflessness."

Wyne Teasdale in *The Mystic Heart* (1999)

In this earth,
In this soil,
In this pure field
Let's not plant any seed
Other than seeds of compassion and love.

Rumi

Divân-e Shams
Ode #1475: 15558

ON SUFI STORIES

I love stories: Sufi stories, Zen stories, Christian parables, folk tales, and proverbs rooted in stories. I am sure this love for stories is shared by all humans because it goes back to our deep history, predating urban life and even writing. Cavemen shared stories when they gathered around the fire; our campfire stories are a continuation of that tradition. In the old days, grandparents told stories to their grandchildren. I was lucky to have had this memorable experience as my father's mother lived with us. And today, parents read bedtime stories to their children from so many books available in bookstores and libraries. Stories found in various cultures and languages constitute an important part of the perennial wisdom of humankind.

In Sufi literature, story plays an important role not only as a teaching tool but also to inspire and strengthen the wayfarer. Sufi stories (*hekâyât*) come in various forms. Some are parables (*amsâl*) such as those Rumi put into verse in his *Masnavi*. Other stories are narratives (*revâyât*) from the lives of renowned sages. For this part of the book, I have translated 12 narratives from Rumi's life; they come from the book of *Manâģeb al-Ârefin* ("The Virtuous Acts of the Mystics") compiled by Ahmad Aflâki in the early fourteenth century. References to the original Persian edition are given at the end of this book. I have translated these stories in a succinct form that reads smoothly in today's English rather than adopting a word-by-word translation of the formal style of classical Persian; nevertheless, the stories and quotes remain true to their original meanings. While Part II of this book presents a selection of Rumi's poems of love and ecstasy, the stories in Part III give a picture of his personal life characterized by compassion and wisdom.

(1)

YOU ARE ALREADY THAT

One day, a man came to Rumi. After their greetings, he started to talk about how he was so fed up with this mundane world and how he wished to go to the hereafter and relax in the presence of the Lord. Rumi said, "What if God is present right here." Then he recited this poem:

> You are a scripture written by God,
> and a mirror reflecting Divine beauty.
> All that exists in the universe is not outside you.
> Seek within. What you seek, you are already that.*

* This poem is found in the quatrains of Rumi (quatrain no. 924 in the Konya manuscript and no. 1921 in Foruzânfar's edition of the *Divân-e Shams*). However, it is also found in the *Mersâd al-Ibâd*, a Persian Sufi book written by Najmuddin Râzi, a contemporary of Rumi who also lived in Anatolia for some years. It is likely that both Rumi and Râzi quoted this poem from an earlier poet in Balkh (probably Majd'eddin Baghdâdi, a Persian Sufi who was a teacher of Râzi and contemporary of Rumi's father Bahâ Valad), but that Rumi's disciples and scribes, hearing it so frequently from Rumi, assumed that it was Rumi's poem and thus entered it in the *Divân-e Shams*.

(2)

HEAVEN AND HELL ARE WITHIN YOU

The following story was told by Bahâuddin Sultan Valad, Rumi's son and successor.

One day, a number of eminent people came to see my father, and he began to speak about spiritual matters in life. Suddenly, he turned to me and said, "Bahâuddin, if you wish to live in paradise on earth, show friendship and kindness to all people and do not keep hatred of anyone in your heart." He then recited this poem:

> I say to myself: Don't put yourself above others.
> Be like a caring drug, not the snake's poisonous fang.
> Do you wish to be safe from the evil-doings of others?
> Don't speak evil!
> Don't mingle with evil-doing people!
> Don't think evil!*

My father continued, "This is because when you think of a friend with love and fondness you become happy, and that happiness is heavenly; but when you remember someone with hostility and bitterness you become sad, and that suffering is like hell. When you think of your loving friends, the orchard of your heart blossoms and is filled with flowers and pleasant fragrance, but when your enemies occupy your mind, your inner garden turns into a desolate place filled with thorns and snakes."

* This poem is in the quatrains of Rumi (quatrain no. 566 in the Konya manuscript and no. 993 in the Foruzânfar edition).

(3)

BE A STRANGER, BE HAPPY

One day, a close friend of Rumi was feeling very sad and depressed with his life. Rumi said to him, "All your worldly sorrows are there because you have set your heart on the world. If you free yourself and feel like a stranger to this world, then you will enjoy seeing all colors and tasting all dishes, without being attached to them, and knowing that you are a passenger. Be like this, and your heart will not be suffocated by worldly sorrows."

(4)

RUMI AND THE ART OF MEDIATION

It is related that one day Rumi was passing through a district of Konya, and saw two men quarrelling fiercely and cursing each other. One of the men said to the other, "If you say one more insulting word to me, you will hear a thousand from me in return." Rumi went over to the men and said, "Please address all your curses to me, for you will hear none in return." The two men came to their senses and made peace in the presence of the Master.

(5)

THE ASCETIC AND HIS BEARD

Who are we to renounce God's creation and the precious gift of life He has given to us? Rumi did not believe in the renunciation of the world. His spirituality was not life-negation but of the kind Jesus recommended: Be ye in the world, but not of it. Sufis usually have families, work and earn their living. The following story is along this line of thought.

One day Rumi along with his disciples and students, having finished their prayers in a mosque, were walking toward downtown Konya. Suddenly an old man, an ascetic with a long grey beard, came over to Rumi to pay his respects. Rumi embraced him and said, "Sir, are you older or your beard?" The monk answered, "Of course, I am older, at least twenty years older than my beard." Rumi then said, "Woe to you! Your beard, which came much later than you, has grown naturally and become mature but you still remain unripe, in the darkness of your thought, and ruining your own life." The monk joined the company of Rumi's disciples.

(6)

WORLDLY DESIRES

It is related that a man came to Rumi and started talking about his financial shortages and complaining about the poor state of his business affairs. Rumi said, "Sir, please leave me at once. Do not make me your friend; then you may attain the friendship of the world and your worldly desires." Rumi then recited the following lines:

> Come; join us, my noble friend!
> Seek neither power nor riches.
> If the Devil himself were like this,
> he would be a king in full splendor.

(7)

LET'S FORGIVE

One day Rumi was in prayer and deep meditation in his room. A man entered the house, begging for food or money. Seeing Rumi in such an absorbed state, the man took a small rug from the room and left. One of Rumi's students, Majd'eddin Marâghi, noticed this, followed the man and found him selling the rug in the market. He caught the man and brought him by force to Rumi's house. After hearing the story, Rumi said, "This man is no thief; he is poor and in need of food. Let's forgive him and buy the rug back from him."

(8)

BE HUMBLE AND KIND

One of the Master's admirable characteristics was that he was humble and kind to all sorts of people – men, women, and children, followers of various faiths or no faith. Once, an Armenian butcher upon seeing Rumi fell to his feet. Rumi respected him in the same manner.

It is also related that a Christian monk from the city of Constantine (Istanbul) had heard of Rumi's fame as a learned man and spiritual master, and wished to meet him. He travelled all the way to Konya. It so happened that the monk saw Rumi on a street in Konya, and went over to him and respectfully prostrated three times. Each time he raised his head he saw Rumi prostrating to him as well.

(9)

DOGS AND THE ART OF COMPASSION

The following story was told by Shaykh Nafis al-Din Sivâsi.

One day, the Master summoned me and gave me two *dirham* (silver) coins to buy sweet bread. In those days, one full tray of sweet bread would cost one *dirham*. I purchased the bread and took it to him. He put all the bread in a bag and left. I became curious and followed him slowly. He went to a ruined building where a dog and several puppies were living. He fed all the bread to the dogs. Upon returning, the Master saw me and said, "This dog can't leave her puppies alone to find food for them because she is afraid that someone would harm her puppies. The good Lord has drawn my attention to their cries and plight."

(10)

A LINGUIST FALLS INTO A WELL

One day Rumi was giving a discourse on spiritual philosophy during which he narrated the following parable.

A linguist had fallen into a well, but he was lucky that a dervish happened to be passing the well and heard the man shouting for help. The dervish called out to other men, saying, "Bring rope, bucket, whatever, so that we can pull this man out." The linguist criticized the dervish that he should have properly said, "Fetch a thick rope and a large bucket." The dervish became silent for a while and then shouted back, "Would you like to remain there until I learn proper syntax?"

The Master then concluded that likewise there are people who have fallen into the well of their worldly position, and all the time they show off their power and fly high in their imagination. But unless they leave these illusions and deeds, and learn from sages, they will not come out of the well they have fallen in.

(11)

WINDOW SHOPPING IN THE SPIRITUAL MARKET

The following story was related by Shamsuddin Malati.

One day, the Master was giving us a discourse in his school and said, "I like Shamsuddin very much, but he has one problem, and I hope that by the grace of God he resolves that problem." I bowed and begged the Master to say what my problem was. He said, "Just because you believe God is present in every being, with this illusion you are running from one person to another." He then recited:

> There are people in human form but with evil traits;
> do not give your hand to any person to guide you.
> Since your eyesight does not penetrate the inside,
> you think that every person has a hidden treasure to offer you.

These words clarified my mind. Indeed, early in my spiritual quest, I used to visit various masters, shaykhs and dervishes, and sought their help and guidance. And since I had the urge of a seeker only, I was running after this and that person. But Master Rumi opened my eye.

On that day, the Master also recited this line over and over so that all of us would remember it by heart:

> In this market-place of drug sellers
> Do no wander hither and thither like jobless people.
> Go to a store which has real medicine, and stay there.*

* These lines are part of a famous ghazal in Rumi's *Divân-e Shams.*

(12)

SAMÂ

One day, Mo'iindeddin Parvâne, the Prime Minister of the Seljuq court in Konya, said to Rumi, "Master, how elegantly you have planted the practice of *samâ** for the whole of humanity."

"No, Sir," Rumi said," I did not plant it. I have harvested it well and have eaten from it."

* Samâ: "Listening" to music and poetry and the performance of spiritual dance in Sufi gatherings.

LAST STORY

In 2009, I visited Rumi's Mausoleum (Mevlana Museum) in Konya, Turkey. Each year, hundreds of thousands of people from various countries visit this historical and spiritual place. The shrine contains not only Rumi's tomb but also the tombs of his family members and closest friends. In the museum, there are displays of the oldest manuscripts of Rumi's poetry books and other items belonging to him or his family. The mausoleum was constructed in 1274 (a year after Rumi died), and has been repaired and expanded from time to time. Capped by a green dome, the building is located in a large garden that was originally the rose-garden of the Seljuq kings in Konya, but since Rumi was buried there, it has become a magnet for his lovers and a lodge for the activities and gatherings of Rumi's Whirling Dervishes. The rose was a favorite flower of Rumi and has a huge presence in his poetry as a symbol of Divine beauty and tenderness of life. The garden is still graced by roses of various colors, and the whole atmosphere of the mausoleum is one of peace and serenity. One can also see cats and kittens which have apparently made the garden their home.

When I saw those cats, I recalled that Rumi was fond of animals and used to keep pet cats. Aflâki writes that during the last week of Rumi's life, one of the cats very near and dear to Rumi, was sensing the illness of the Master and was frequently mewing loudly. Rumi commented, "Do you know what this poor cat is saying? She is saying to me: You are leaving this world for a higher realm and returning to the original home. But what am I going to do here? Don't leave me alone." Everyone cried when they heard these words. It is related that after Rumi passed away, the cat stopped eating and drinking for a whole week and eventually died. Rumi's daughter, Malakeh Khâtun, wrapped her in a coffin and buried the body near Rumi's tomb.

TERMS AND SYMBOLS IN RUMI'S POETRY

Âtash: Fire. The burning, melting, and transforming quality of love. Fire in reference to love has a positive connotation in Rumi's poetry, but when fire is associated with passion, lust, and greed, it has a negative, resentful meaning.

Baǧa ("Subsistence"): Real being; living as a human awakened to reality and in the presence of the eternal Beloved. In Sufi teachings, this stage comes after *fanâ*.

Beloved (*maa'shuǧ, duust, yâr, jânâ*): God or its reflection of love and beauty in the entire creation including humans.

Body (*tan, badan, jesm*): The physical body rooted in soil (*gel*) and water (*âb*). While Rumi does not recommend ascetic practices harmful to the human body and health, he shows strong contempt for a life of attachments to physical lust. In this sense, he regards flesh as a veil to reality, and contrasts it with an awakened, spiritual life.

Davrish (Turkish pronunciation: *Dervish*): "Standing at the door (*dar*)," implying a fakir (poor, beggar) who practices spiritual poverty. A Sufi in a general sense.

Divân-e Shams: *Divân* means "poetry book" and every eminent Persian poet has a *divân* named after him. Rumi dedicated his book of poetry to his soul friend Shams-e Tabrizi. Also called *Divân-e Kabir* ("The Great Book of Poetry"), it contains over 3200 lyric odes (*ghazal*) and about 1800 quatrains (*rubâiyât*) which Rumi started to compose in 1244, at age 37 when he met Shams, and continued it until his death in 1273.

Dûvâne, Sheydâ, Majnun: Love-mad

Drunk (*mast*): One who is selfless (*bi'khod*), senseless (*bi'hush*), and absorbed (*maj'zub*) in the Beloved. This spiritual intoxication comes from the joy and love of the Beloved.

Ecstasy (*vajd, shuur*): An overwhelming, selfless feeling of joy that results from a spiritual experience such as in music and dance.

Eshǧ: Love

Fanâ ("Annihiliation"): Similar to the Buddhist concept of nirvana, *fanâ* is the extinction of the ego (carnal self) and self-centered desires and greed. After this stage, the seeker lives in *baqa*.

Friend (*duust, yâr*): See "Beloved"

Garden (*bâgh*), Rose-garden (*golzâr, golestân*): The physical garden, home to flowers, trees, fruits and greenery, is a landscape of beauty, fragrance, serenity, mystery, and unity displayed in diversity. So is the spiritual garden, according to Sufi poetry. It symbolizes the heart or an inner space where the true human nature, Divine spirit, beauty, peace, joy and mystery are manifest. The notion of "garden" goes back to the Persian *pardis* (from which the word "paradise" has come), a walled garden that has been a salient feature of civilization in Iran.

Haqq: "Truth." In Sufi literature, it is identified with God as the only eternal reality and the source of all existence and intellect.

Heart (*del, qalb*): A symbolic organ for the human spirit; the inner space for pure consciousness, joy and love; the garden of spiritual secrets; the inner mirror that reflects Divine attributes; the field of spiritual experience; inner voice; the seat of conscience and human's true nature. Just as the physical heart is essential to our biological function, the spiritual heart plays a vital role in our inner journey and enlightenment – hence its prominent place in Rumi's poetry.

Jân, Ravân: Soul; life energy.

Khamush: Silent, Silence. Some scholars believe that *Khamush* is one of Rumi's pen-names as he has often used this word in the last line of many of his sonnets (*ghazal*) in the *Divân-e Shams*.

Khezr (Arabic pronunciation: *Khidhr*; "Green Man"): A legendary prophet or spiritual master in Sufi literature who found the Water of Life and guides the wayfarers to it.

Khodâ: God.

Khayâl (also pronounced *khyâl*): Image, imagination. Sometimes, it has a positive connotation as in the Beloved's image or spiritual vision, and sometimes negative as in our illusionary perceptions.

Masnavi (Arabic pronunciation: *Mathnawi*): "Couplet." It is a form of poetry in which two lines rhyme (hence a couplet) but the rhyme changes from one couplet to another throughout the poem. Masnavi is usually a long poem (tens of couplets). Rumi used this poetic form in composing his book *Masnavi-ye Maa'navi* ('Spiritual Couplets'), which consists of six volumes of parables in verse (totaling about 25,000 couplets) and was composed during the last decade of Rumi's life. This book is so well known that it is simply called the *Masnavi*.

Mawlânâ (Arabic), Mowlânâ (Persian), Mevlânâ (Turkish): "Our Master." A respectful title for Rumi which has been used by the Eastern peoples for centuries.

Moon (*mah, mâh*), Moonlight (*mah'tâb*): A recurring image in classical Persian poetry for the beauty of the Beloved, especially when its shining light is viewed in the backdrop of the dark night.

Nafs: Carnal self; ego

Non-existence, Nothingness, Emptiness, Void (*adam, niistii*): (1) Rumi often uses this word to indicate the mysterious origin and common home of all things in the world. While the phenomena are visible and perishable (subject to change and destruction), the realm of non-existence is invisible, eternal, and sourced in the Divine. In Rumi's view, creation is a continual coming into existence of phenomena from this formless, colorless, unified realm. (2) The perishable (*niistii*) nature of the visible existence. (3) The death and annihilation of the carnal self (ego); same as *fanâ*, which is an ideal feature of the spiritual journey.

Nur, Roshani: Light. This word has a rich symbolism such as Divine manifestation, the unveiling of reality and spiritual truth, or the quality of knowing and seeing. It is sometimes contrasted with "darkness" (*zolomat, târiiki*).

Ocean or Sea (*bahr, daryâ*): The infinite vastness and mysterious foundation, of existence, the hidden, inner reality beyond appearances (symbolized as foam or froth, *kaf*) and phenomena (waves, *mowj*).

Poverty (*faqr*): Spiritual poverty, not-attachment to worldly wealth (materialism) and greed (egoism).

Reed (*ney*): The reed flute was a favorite musical instrument of Rumi and appears frequently in his poetry as a symbol for the pure, enlightened human being who sings with a lamenting voice in this mundane world because (s)he feels separated from the source (reed bed) and yearns for union with the Beloved.

Rose (*gol*): The word *gol* means both flower and rose which is a remarkable feature of Persian gardens and is a recurring image in its poetry. Rose symbolizes the beauty, serenity and joyfulness of life in the presence of the Beloved. The flower is rooted in the earth, grows together with its thorns, and shares its beauty and fragrance even though for a short span of its life. In some ways, the rose has the same symbolism as that of the lotus in Buddhism and Hinduism.

Rubâ'ii (plural: *Rubâiyât*): Quatrain; a four-line poem in which the first, second and fourth lines rhyme.

Ruh: Spirit; the Divine essence ("breath") in humans.

Sâgi ("Cupbearer"): An important symbol in classical Persian poetry for a beautiful woman who serves wine and shares her pleasant, friendly presence with lovers and drinkers. *Sâgi* thus plays an important role in our awakening from the ego and mundane affairs to the heart and inner reality and beauty.

Samâ (Turkish pronunciation: *Sema*): "Audition." The Sufi practice of listening to or performing music and songs (often poems); it is sometimes associated with dance such as the whirling dance in the Mevlevi (Rumi's) tradition.

Seeker (*tâleb*, *juuyande*): One who searches for spiritual truth, the real self, and enlightenment.

Showq, *Eshtiyâq*: Longing for the Beloved or the original home.

Shuur: Frenzy, love-madness.

Sufi: A person who follows the mystical, spiritual path historically developed in the Islamic world (Middle East, Central Asia, South Asia, and North Africa). There are a number of Sufi orders and lineages, such as Mevlevi (Mawlavviya) Order named after Rumi.

Sun (*khorshid*, *shams*), Sunshine (*aftâb*): A widely-used symbol for the source of brightness, warmth, vision, knowing, and enlightened life. Shams-e Tabrizi, a wandering dervish from the city of Tabriz in northern Iran, was Rumi's soul friend; in his poems, Rumi often uses the name Shams in association with the qualities of the Sun (*shams*).

Tavern (*kharâbât*): A place, usually in a ruined (*kharâb*) suburb area, where people drink wine and get drunk on the premises. This symbol is widely used in Sufi poetry for a situation in which the seeker becomes detached from the mundane world, drinks from the Divine wine, and transcends the egoistic life.

Union (*vesâl*): Spiritual homecoming; union with the Beloved.

Vahdat: Unity, union, oneness.

Vahdat-e Vojuud (Oneness of Being, Unity of Existence): A prominent concept in the Sufi teachings of Ibn Arabi, Rumi and other masters, it means the unity, interconnectedness and common source of all existence (unity in multiplicity). It also implies the existence of One Reality (God) and its manifestation throughout the created world.

Veil (*hejâb*) or Curtain (*parde*): That which conceals reality from us. In many spiritual traditions, the veil is identified with our own greedy ego and self-centered, twisted perceptions.

Water of Life (*âb-e hayât*, *âb-e zendegi*): A symbol for a state of being awakened to the spiritual heart and the Divine reality of existence. Whoever drinks from the water of life attains immortality, which in Sufi terms, means a life in *baqâ*.

Wayfarer (*sâlek*, *rah'ro*): One who has embarked on a spiritual journey.

Whirling (Persian: *charkh-zani*): A spiritual dance practiced by the Whirling Dervishes. Rumi himself performed whirling dance as part of the *samâ*, but the practice was formalized by his son Sultan Valad.

Wine (*mey*, *bâde*, *sharâb*): A recurring image in Persian Sufi poetry which represents the nectar of love and realization of selflessness (transcending the ego).

Zikr (Arabic pronunciation: *Dhikr*): "Remembrance." A Sufi practice of chanting or saying in silence certain words or prayers such as the names of God as a way to mindfulness and meditative mood. The practice of *Zikr* is necessary because the worldly, egoistic life makes us forgetful of the One Reality in the world and in our inner being. Remembrance (mindfulness) connects us to this source of love, joy, strength, and creativity.

Zolf (lock of hair, ringlet): It has various meanings according to the context of the poem. The long, black, curved hair of the Beloved oftentimes symbolizes the mysterious, charming character of the manifested world, through which the seeker is drawn to the Beloved.

The tree's branch draws water
from the lowermost point upward.
In the same way, love uplifts our soul
without any need for a ladder.

Rumi

Diván-e Shams
Ode #1940: 20472

SOURCES AND BIBLIOGRAPHY

For the quatrains of Rumi, I used the following two sources:

Foruzânfar Edition (F)
Mowlânâ Jalâluddin Mohammad Balkhi Rumi, *Kulliyât-e Shams* (*Divân-e Kabir*), edited by Badi al-Zamân Foruzânfar (Tehran University Press, 1957-1967; reprinted by Amir Kabir Press, 1976), 10 volumes (volume 8 contains the quatrains).

Konya Manuscript, Printed Edition (K)
Mowlânâ Jalâluddin Mohammad Balkhi Rumi, *Divân-e Kabir: Kulliyât-e Shams-e Tabrizi*, with introduction, footnotes and indexes by Towfiĝ H. Sob'hâni (Tehran: Anjoman-e Âsâr va Mafâkher-e Farhangi, 2007), 2 volumes.

The numbers of the translated quatrains from the above two sources are given below.

Quatrain	F	K
Page 5	1881	1002

Part II. The Rubaiyat (Quatrains) of Rumi:
144+1 Poems on the Art of Living

(1) On the Pain and Joy of Longing

	F	K
1	17	16
2	142	1223
3	479	1543
4	547	483
5	566	469

6	581	384
7	788	395
8	894	509
9	1269	680
10	1273	1731
11	1321	689
12	1611	865

(2) The Search

13	32	1172
14	138	1332
15	369	1240
16	702	339
17	838	293
18	863	1498
19	1438	1581
20	1557	890
21	1601	849
22	1734	1047
23	1864	1838
24	1975	1100

(3) Who Am I?

25	15	40
26	16	1177
27	334	1247
28	363	1252
29	366	1259
30	532	326
31	664	242
32	1085	1377
33	1552	883
34	1655	848
35	1905	1860
36	1910	1078

(4) The Beloved's Face

37	14	1164
38	146	1337
39	264	206
40	265	1751
41	304	141
42	351	118

43	460	1505
44	776	456
45	802	1816
46	1019	581
47	1257	707
48	1776	939

(5) Die to Yourself

49	20	7
50	38	34
51	51	33
52	101	56
53	206	70
54	271	1346
55	367	165
56	1095	612
57	1151	1408
58	1254	644
59	1816	1083
60	1937	1142

(6) The Art of Living

61	23	21
62	225	197
63	288	145
64	462	342
65	593	392
66	693	256
67	1077	602
68	1153	692
69	1518	816
70	1501	780
71	1420	807
72	644	404

(7) Nigh Secrets

73	7	3
74	11	1165
75	58	18
76	98	47
77	456	1809
78	771	402
79	780	420

80	1164	687
81	1186	686
82	1634	1605
83	1648	870
84	1783	1037

(8) Water of Life

85	6	31
86	18	1152
87	31	1157
88	522	1654
89	834	387
90	951	511
91	1081	1381
92	1152	627
93	1343	1708
94	1365	678
95	1564	892
96	1630	872

(9) Fire of Love

97	9	8
98	49	28
99	147	180
100	226	147
101	387	1224
102	449	1639
103	754	434
104	1046	1364
105	1078	1379
106	1083	611
107	1323	1402
108	1485	823

(10) Unity and Union

109	19	1153
110	46	17
111	319	116
112	321	71
113	322	90
114	650	225
115	731	259
116	800	361

117	830	394
118	1070	606
119	1632	873
120	1633	856

(11) Peaceful Mind

121	25	25
122	57	1154
123	386	65
124	395	61
125	441	455
126	544	467
127	631	474
128	636	396
129	805	359
130	900	494
131	993	566
132	1332	726

(12) Rumi on His Life, Poetry and Death

133	681	288
134	600	389
135	616	362
136	914	499
137	1293	727
138	1143	1705
139	1206	736
140	508	252
141	839	352
142	1284	1714
143	791	349
144	519	1791

Last Poem

145	795	298

Part III. Compassion & Wisdom in Action:
    12+1 Stories from Rumi's Life

Shamsuddin Ahmad Aflâki (death 1356), *Manâĝeb al-Ârefîn* ("The Virtuous Acts of the Mystics," in Persian), edited by Tahsin Yazichi, 2 volumes (Ankara: Turk Tarih Kurumu Basimeri, 1976-1980, 2nd edition; reprinted in Tehran: Donyâ-ye Kitâb, 1983)

ACKNOWLEDGMENTS

It was my school books and Persian teachers who first introduced me to Rumi's poetry. Selected poems from Rumi and other Persian poets were included in our language and literature textbooks. And in those classes, not only did we have to learn to write the poems accurately in Persian as the teacher dictated, but also we had to memorize the poems and recite them by heart and explain in prose what the verses meant. Those were not always easy things, and some lines did not make sense to us – the young boys who were more dedicated to playing soccer and hanging out. I remember one of my teachers once said, "When Rumi composed these poems he was not a school boy but a mature man and a master poet. When you reach his age, you will appreciate these poems. Be patient. For now, just memorize the poems and get good grades." I do not claim to have reached that mature, masterly understanding of Rumi's poetry, but how true my teacher's words were: I find these Persian poems so enjoyable and inspiring that I would like to share some of them with English readers in this little book. Over the years, I have also read books from a number of historians, commentators, and translators who have deepened my knowledge of Rumi's life, work and poetic vision. I should especially mention Badi al-Zamân Foruzânfar, Jalâl Homâ'ii, Reynold Nicholson, Arthur John Arberry, Abdulbâqi Golpinarli, Abdol Hossein Zarrinkub, Annemarie Schimmel, William Chittick, Towfiĝ Sob'hâni, Hassan Lâhuti, and Franklin Lewis. I have been fortunate to have met many good friends who also appreciate poetry as nourishing food for the human soul and culture. I would like to express my gratitude to Florin Nielsen, a teacher, poet, friend and a Rumi lover, who kindly read the entire manuscript of this book and suggested valuable comments that improved the text. Any error is, however, mine.

ABOUT THE POET

The Persian poet Jalâluddin Rumi (1207-1273) is regarded as one of the greatest mystical poets and sages of all time, and English translations of his works are currently among the most widely-read poems. Rumi's poetry books include the *Divân-e Shams* and the *Masnavi*, which express in rich imagery the journey of the soul on the path of love and the joy of love in our life and in the entire world.

ABOUT THE TRANSLATOR

Rasoul Shams first learned of Rumi's poems in his Persian classes as a young boy growing up in Iran. The works of Rumi and other Persian poets have been his spiritual companions for over three decades. His life and education are rooted in both East and West. He is currently translating another Rumi anthology from the original sources.

ABOUT THE PUBLISHER

RUMI PUBLICATIONS are an imprint of the Rumi Poetry Club, founded in 2007 on the occasion of the eight hundredth anniversary of Rumi's birth to foster literature and art that nourish the human spiritual life and enrich our global culture. We celebrate inspirational words and perennial wisdom. For more information visit our website:

www.rumipoetryclub.com

Made in the USA
Charleston, SC
30 December 2014